T0147916

To GOD BE THE GLORY

Russell George

Order this book online at www.trafford.com
or email orders@trafford.com

Most Trafford titles are also available at major online book retailers.

All Scripture quotations are taken from the King James Version of the Bible.

Printed in the United States of America.

ISBN: 978-1-4669-6778-6 (sc)
ISBN: 978-1-4669-6773-1 (e)

Trafford rev. 11/05/2012

 www.trafford.com

North America & international
toll-free: 1 888 232 4444 (USA & Canada)
phone: 250 383 6864 ♦ fax: 812 355 4082

Contents

Pictures

Preface

Please don't think I'm writing my life story in anticipation of becoming famous. To the contrary, it will most likely reveal what a fool I am for thinking anyone will read it. Time will tell.

For some time I debated about whether I should write the story of my life. I didn't want to write even one sentence if it was just to draw attention to myself. This book is a testimony to the glorious things that God has done. To God be the glory! Great things he has done! He took an insignificant Nebraska farm boy to the mission field in Argentina. This is the story of how God worked in my life, first of all to make me an instrument he could use, then to make me willing to be used, and then of how he has used me. What he did for me he can do for you.

I don't offer myself as an example of obedience, efficiency or accomplishment. In many ways I failed. Many things I could have done better. Altogether too often I have taken glory to myself that should have been given to God. Since this is a book about what God did for me, there is no way I can write it and leave myself out of it. If God is glorified through the pages of this book, I have accomplished what I set out to do. If it just brings glory to me, then I have been a miserable failure.

The omniscience of God goes far beyond our comprehension. I stand in awe of what God has done. I can only say, "He planned it all." From eternity past he has a plan for our lives. The extent to which he can carry out that plan depends on our willingness to surrender our lives to him so he can do his will in and through us. God has given freedom of the will to all. This would be a perfect world if every living soul would surrender his will to the will of God. We are given freedom of the will so that God can be glorified. God is glorified by human beings. God wouldn't receive any glory if we didn't have liberty to choose to glorify him. According to Isaiah 43:7 God made us for his glory. "Even everyone that is called by my name: for I have created him for my glory, I have formed him; yea, I have made him." It is my prayer that this book will be used of God to motivate you to take heed to the exhortation of Proverbs 3:5-6. "Trust in the Lord with all thine heart; and lean not unto thine own understanding. In all thy ways acknowledge him, and he shall direct thy paths."

Acknowledgments

I want to express my gratitude to the following for proofreading my manuscript.

Dr. and Mrs. Jack Cribbs

Rev. and Mrs Ronald McLucas

Rev. Kenneth Steward

Dorothy Selden

Debra George

I am also indebted to my wife, Margaret, for her input and suggestions.

Childhood Experiences

Childhood Experience

I was born in a little farm house south of Aurora, Nebraska. I was the first child born to Emery and Eunice George. My family consisted of 4 sisters: Reta, Twilla, Iona, and Beth. I had one brother, Harley Ray, who drowned in a stock tank when he was only 3 years old. Before I was old enough to remember any thing, my parents and grandparents moved to a farm near Ericson, Nebraska.

God sometimes takes years to prepare his servants. The Bible says in Esther 4:14 "Who knoweth whether thou art come to the kingdom for such a time as this?" God knew that, in my case at least, it would be best for me to be reared as a farm boy. Many of God's servants grew up on a farm. Out in the Sand Hills of Nebraska I was sheltered from the wicked influence of city life. We didn't have television. In fact, we didn't even have a radio until I was, perhaps seven or eight years old. John Sloan, a bachelor neighbor, was one of the first in our neighborhood to get a radio. He and his mother invited us to come up to their house to listen to the radio. We went one Sunday afternoon. We sat there for about two hours doing nothing but listening to the radio. No one said a word. After that, my parents decided they should buy a radio too. It was an exciting day when my Dad brought home our first radio. Since we didn't have electricity, it came with a big battery that sat behind it to give it power. I helped my mother string up a wire

3

outside for an antenna. I didn't understand what that had to do with it. For months after that we rushed to finish the chores at night, so we could listen to the radio. Some of our favorite programs were Fibber McGee and Molly, and Amos and Andy.

God knew that I would need to learn the significance of what the Bible says in Luke 12:15. "A man's life consisteth not in the abundance of the things which he possesseth." I was born in the waning years of the great depression. I don't recall hearing my parents complain about being poor. Possibly it was because the economy was improving. By today's standards, we lived in extreme poverty. There was always food on the table and we had clothes on our backs. What more could we ask for?

We didn't have electricity, but there was always a supply of kerosene for the lamps. We called it "coal oil" back then. We didn't have a refrigerator, but there was always fresh milk each day because we milked the cows. Every time we went into town we brought back two or three packages of frozen meat from the locker box. We didn't have a bathroom in our house, but we had a path that led to a shack. Inside was a bench with two holes in it. There was also a roll of toilet paper, or more often, an old Sears catalogue. There was a hook and eye screw to lock the door for privacy. What more was needed? God knew the time would come when I would need to be willing to give up some of the luxuries of life, and be able to do it without feeling like I was falling off a cliff.

God, in his mercy, gave me parents who had some moral convictions. My parents never smoked or drank. If a dirty word ever came out of our mouths, we could expect to be disciplined by one of two wooden candle sticks that always sat on the buffet in our dining room.

On a farm there was always work to be done. There were cows to milk, eggs to gather, as well as chickens, pigs, and calves to feed. In the summer there were always weeds to hoe in the garden. I enjoyed going to the field with my dad, and following along behind as he planted and cultivated corn with a team of horses. When we came in at noon he would let me lead one of the horses to the tank to get a drink. Later in the summer it was time to mow, rake, and stack hay. I enjoyed riding on the back of the sweep. That was a big wooden fork, pulled by two horses, which my Dad used to bring in load after load of hay, and deposited it on the big fork of the stacker. Then a team of horses pulled a cable that lifted the big fork up and dumped the hay on the stack in formation. At first my mother stacked the hay. As I got older that became my job. I was having fun. No one told me that it was called "work."

Another exiting day for me was when the threshing crew came to our farm to thrash the grain. I watched as the owner of the thrashing machine parked it in a field and put on the long belt between the machine and the tractor. The big machine began to roar and vibrate, as dust and straw belched out of the straw stacker. I felt like a man when I helped the men pitch bundles on a rack, and then pitch them into the machine.

Work Experiences

Work Experiences

My first work experience was at home, helping my Dad on the farm. I was fortunate in that I grew up on the farm. It's an education in itself. Being close to nature teaches us a lot. I also learned a lot of practical lessons from my Dad. He was a hard worker. He and my mother nearly always had the cows milked in the morning before I got out of bed.

My earliest memories were of living in a little two room wood frame house on my grandfather's farm. My dad and grandfather farmed the place together. About a block away, up a steep hill, sat my grandparent's two story house. I still remember my mother climbing that hill with a pail, to bring water from the well that was just outside the door of my grandparent's house. On wash days she had to make several trips to get enough water to fill the wash tub. She heated water on the kitchen wood burning stove. Just a short distance from the house was the chicken house. It was what was called a straw shed. The frame was made of chicken wire that was filled with straw. Then more chicken wire was stretched across the tree branches that formed the roof, and it was covered with straw.

When I was about five years old my parents rented a farm about a mile away. There we had a five room house with running water. Several days were spent in moving. I went with my mother when she drove the team and wagon moving things to our new house. On one trip she moved the chickens. They were all put in the wagon that was covered with chicken wire, so they couldn't fly out.

It was on the farm that I learned the discipline of work. It was often my job to gather the eggs in the evening. Other jobs were:

1. Filling fruit baskets with cobs each evening to burn in the stove. They were picked up in the chicken yard and the pig pen.
2. Going to the pasture to bring in the cows to be milked in the evening.
3. Going to the pasture in the morning to bring in the horses to be harnessed for their day's work.

As I grew older I learned to milk cows, pitch hay and manure, turn the separator to separate the cream from the milk, and carry the skim milk to the calves that were bucket fed. What remained was given to the pigs.

I learned perseverance and hard work from my dad. Often I went with him to bring a load of hay from one of the hay stacks. When we had the hay rack full he would often say, "Well, I expect that's about enough." I was ready to quit, but he would throw on another twenty or more forks full. In my early teens he lost his right hand in a hammer mill. That is a machine used on a farm to grind grain. Some wondered if he could go on completing his farm work with only one hand; but he did.

My first job away from home was helping a farmer during corn picking time. He had a tractor mounted corn picker. The first day I was riding in the wagon that was pulled behind the tractor and pushing the corn to the back of the wagon. When he came to the end of the row he turned to go back on a different row. I was standing in the front of the wagon, and the chute that threw the corn into the wagon came around and hit me in the side of my head. I saw a few stars, but fortunately I wasn't hurt. The farmer didn't see what happened and I never told him. My job was to unload the wagon while he went out and filled another one. With the money I earned on that job I bought a single shot rifle that I saw advertised in the Sears catalogue.

In the final days of high school I saw an ad in the Nebraska Farmer Magazine. It was placed there by a farmer in western Nebraska, who was looking for a farm hand. I wrote to him, and he hired me. My parents took me to Grand Island, where I boarded a train that took me to Bridgeport. There the farmer was waiting for me. While there I slept in a bunk house and ate my meals with the family. I had an experience there that I'll never forget. My boss asked me to take a potato planter back that he had borrowed from another farmer. I was pulling it with a little Ford tractor. I was driving along the highway enjoying the scenery when, all at once, the left rear wheel of the tractor fell off and lay in the oncoming lane of traffic. I could hear what sounded like a truck coming up the hill on the other side. I knew I had to get that tire off the road immediately because the driver of the truck wouldn't have time to stop before he hit it. A super dose of adrenalin must have kicked in to enable me to move that heavy tire. The driver of the truck stopped and took me to the farm down the road, where he was going to make a delivery. There I called my boss and he came to my rescue. After about six weeks of working there my boss sent me back home. I wasn't man enough to handle the fifty pound sacks of potatoes that he expected me to move. I went back home and got a job helping a rancher with his hay harvest.

I worked two other summers for ranchers helping them with their hay harvest. They were seasonal jobs, but they gave me some money for my college expenses. The second summer, when the harvest was finished, the rancher took me back to Bartlett, the town where I went to high school. There I called my Dad and asked him to come after me. While I was waiting for him, I went into the bank and started talking to Bob Martin, the cashier at the bank. He also was the proprietor of an agricultural business. He asked me if I would like to work for him. Before my dad arrived, I had a job. Bob had been a World War II Air Force pilot. He had a small plane and was doing aerial crop spraying.

Exciting things started happening in my life. Bob rented a room for me at the local motel. One of the two restaurants in town was just around the corner from the motel so I had a place to eat. Just a few days after I started working for Bob, Herbie Thomas came looking for me. He was the county clerk at the courthouse. He had a car he wanted to sell me. As I recall, he was selling the car to settle the estate of his deceased father. It was a 1939 Chevy and it became my first car. I was thrilled with it! I couldn't wait to go out home and show it to my parents.

I was fascinated with airplanes and loved every minute of being around the plane. Bob got me up early in the morning to go out to spray corn fields to kill grass hoppers. He showed me how to hold up a white flag on a pole at the end of the field, to mark where he was supposed to fly. He would fly just a few feet over my head with a thundering roar. While he ascended and turned around, I walked down 14 more rows and held up the flag again. Sometimes Bob took me up for a ride in the plane. That was a thrill!

By mid morning Bob flew the plane back to the hanger and went to work at the bank. I drove his pickup back into town and kept busy with jobs around the hanger, while he was working at the bank. One job was to wash the bug stains off the leading edges of the wings of the plane and the windshield. By 4:00 in the afternoon Bob was ready to spray more crops. I had mixed the insecticide and had the tank full on the plane. I had also filled the fuel tank. I drove out to the farm and waited for him to come with the plane.

Bob also had two self propelled combines. Farmers paid him to harvest alfalfa seed. He would go out with the plane and spray defoliant on the field, so it would be all dried up and ready for the harvest a week later. He taught me how to run one of the combines. After harvesting the seed we took it back to the hanger and spread it on the floor to dry. When it was dry we ran it through a seed cleaner he had installed in the hanger. After that it was bagged and ready for the farmer to sell. In the fall we put corn heads on the combines and started harvesting corn.

A Good Education

Russell when he graduated
From High School

A Good Education

God knew that his servant would need a good education. That is why, in his providence, I was privileged to attend a one room country school. Some might consider that as a disadvantage, but that's because we are inclined to think that modern is always better. That's not always true. Some of our forefathers had a good education. How did they get it? They were not the product of our modern education systems. If they had a college education, it's very possible that it was superior to the education our colleges offer today.

The local farmers served on the school board of the one room country school. They hired and fired the teachers. Before a teacher made any major decisions she consulted with the president of the school board. The school day started at 9:00 in the morning with the Pledge of Allegiance to the flag. After that we sang a patriotic song like "God Bless America" or "The Star Spangled Banner". Then we settled down to study time or recitations. Every morning and afternoon there was a 15 minute recreation time that we called a "recess." We had an hour off at noon. Part of that time was spent eating our lunch that we carried to school with us each day. The other part of the noon hour was spent playing games in the school yard.

In the one room school there were no classes in human sciences. There was no political indoctrination. Oh, yes, the teachers encouraged us to read the newspaper and be aware of what was going on in the world. Most of the time was spent in reading, writing, and solving mathematical equations. I enjoyed acting in the school programs we always had each year for Halloween, Thanksgiving, or Christmas. All the neighbors gathered at the school that night. The room was illuminated by kerosene lamps mounted on the walls. After the program there was a box social. The ladies prepared a box of food and decorated it. The boxes were sold at auction to the men. They ate the food with the woman or girl who prepared it. Wives always made sure their husband would recognize their box. The money was often used by the school to buy athletic equipment.

I can't blame the public school system entirely for failing to give children a good education. Some of the blame falls on the parents for failing to teach their children to be obedient. They tell me that now children start in kindergarten and, for the first time, they are told there are things they can't do. Rather than accept it, sometimes they fight, kicking and screaming. When our children were little, the philosophy on child raising was that you shouldn't use corporal discipline on your child, because it might warp his tender little personality. We didn't buy it. It's not that we didn't have any struggles, but we saw good results from spanking them when it was needed. Our children are all gainfully employed. None have ever been on welfare. None have been in prison. None have drawn unemployment checks. All attend church faithfully. It pays to take heed to Proverbs

22:6 that says "Train up a child in the way he should go: and when he is old, he will not depart from it."

In our day, many enter college at a disadvantage because our modern educational systems are failing to equip our young people with the basic knowledge they need in reading, writing, and arithmetic. I'm convinced that I graduated from high school with an education far superior to today's average high school graduate.

I was never at the head of my class. Others had higher IQ's than I did. In my first years of grade school I frustrated my teachers many times. Maybe that's why I had to repeat the first grade. Often, when I was called upon to give my reading assignment in class, I burst into tears and couldn't finish it. I couldn't give my teacher a reason why. I'm not sure if it was because I was timid, or because of an inferiority complex.

High school was a unique experience for me. In those days the county couldn't afford to run buses to the ranches to pick up students. Some lived as much as 30 miles away. Therefore the high school had dormitories for the boys and the girls. We stayed there Monday through Thursday nights. Parents brought their children into town Monday morning and came after them Friday after school was out. For my sisters and me, it was our first experience of being away from home. We soon learned how to get along with others.

Meals were served in the dining hall at the girl's dorm. Sometimes we had kitchen duty; most often for breakfast. Sometimes it was setting the tables. At other times it was frying pancakes or French toast. After the evening meal we had to wash the dishes.

The upper classmen liked to show their authority by picking on the freshmen. They were enthralled if they could get us freshmen to kick, fight or cuss them. I soon learned that the best way to get them to leave me alone was to do the humiliating things they asked me to do, without any serious resentment. They didn't get any thrills out of that.

The dorm matron had her room just inside the front door. There was one matron who's name was Mrs. Clark and another was Mrs. Kenan. We exasperated the dorm matrons by blowing out a fuse at night. We found an easy way to do it. We would shut a light off in one of our rooms, and then we took the light bulb out and stuck a coat hanger in the socket. When we flipped the switch the lights went out in the whole dorm. We snickered under our breath as we listened for the dorm matron to come out with her flashlight and replace the fuse. About a half hour later another fuse would burn out. I don't think she ever learned what was causing the fuses to burn out.

After the evening meal the tables were all cleared in the dining hall and we gathered around the tables for an hour of supervised study time. The local Methodist church had a service on Wednesday evening for anyone who wanted to go. A lady from the church came to the school and chaperoned us on the three block walk to the church and back. I often went because it meant I could get out of the study hall. I didn't take anything very seriously that I heard at church. It was there that I heard for the first time some of the old hymns that are still precious to me.

I made some good friends during my high school years. Two of my best friends were Fred Potts and Herb Mignery. We sometimes went to one another's home over the weekend. I had my first infatuation with a girl at that time. Her name was Marge. We had a few dates, but it never became serious.

In my high school days I developed a love for reading. The school library was just a little hole in the wall. The door to the library was also the check out desk. One of the girls in school was often the librarian. I read most all of the western novels in the library. While other boys were shooting baskets at the gym, I spent my time reading. No doubt it helped build my vocabulary.

Gym class was a requirement, but I never took much interest in athletics. I didn't have the physique for strenuous athletics. I did enjoy going to the basketball games and looked forward to the track meets in the spring. I ran the mile race one year, but I didn't win.

Like most senior high school students, I spent time thinking about what I wanted to do with my life. I had several aspirations. Some times I dreamed about being a big rancher. Then I thought about being a veterinarian. After graduating from high school I enrolled in the University of Nebraska with intentions of being a vocational agriculture teacher. My aspirations and dreams never included the most remote thought of the way I have spent my life. I look forward to telling you about that later.

Many young people think it's important to get a good education in order that they might make a lot of money. The reason for seeking to get a good education should be to enable one to live a successful life. Making money is just a part of it. Success in life consists in helping others have a happy life. It's possible to be rich and hurt more people than you have helped.

No one has a good education if he doesn't have a basic knowledge of the Bible. Knowing what God says in his Word and obeying it will enable you to be a success in life. Being a success in life, in turn, glorifies God. God's purpose in putting us here is for his glory. Isaiah 43:7 says "Even every one that is called by my name: for I have created him for my glory, I have formed him; yea, I have made him."

Turning Points

The Great Turning Point In My Life

Being a college student was a trying experience for me. At the same time, it was a turning point in my life. My parents took me to Lincoln and situated me in my dormitory at the University of Nebraska. I felt like a fish must feel when it's out of water. I was in a dormitory with 700 men. I didn't know anyone. I was too much of an introvert to make friends, but God had mercy on me. He sent a young man from the room next door to ask if he could borrow some ink. His name was Dean Hansen. We soon became friends. He invited me to accompany him and his room mate to the dining hall for the evening meal.

Before I go on, I need to explain a strange repulsion I had for anything spiritual. I'm sure this experience was not unique with me. After working with people for many years I have found a lot of people with repugnance for anything spiritual. They don't really know why. They can't explain it. They can't give an intelligent reason for it. It is just something they feel an urge to turn away from. I seldom heard my parents speak with disdain about spiritual truths. It was just something they didn't talk about. Occasionally I heard neighbor boys tell dirty jokes about spiritual matters.

Neighbors all around us lived as if there was no God. I thought, "If people can live without God, why should I bother with it?" I made up my mind that I had no need or time for it. I was what could be called an "atheist," but I didn't know what that word meant. When I was a child, the only times we appeared in church were for weddings or funerals.

The only one who ever talked to me about my soul was a man by the name of Charlie Bowman. Everyone knew that Charlie had a mental problem. He was a tramp who came through the neighborhood from time to time. Some of the neighbors would give him some food and a place to stay for a few nights in exchange for some odd jobs. Once he was at a neighbor's house when I was there. He talked to me about my need of Christ. I passed it off as though it were some nonsense that someone put in his shallow brain.

The next experience that I recall happened when I was a freshman in high school. I was in a science class in the basement of the girl's dormitory. One of the Gideons came through and gave all of us a pocket New Testament. I left mine lying on the desk in front of me through the remainder of the class. When the class was over I gathered up my books and carried the New Testament to the bottom of the stairs. There was an empty metal waste basket there. I threw my New Testament in that waste basket. It was as though something pierced my heart when I heard it hit the bottom of that empty waste basket. Never-the-less, I went on my way thinking I had made good riddance of that detestable New Testament.

God, in his mercy, spared me from the depths of immorality. I was blessed by having parents that never drank nor smoked. I have never tasted a drop of whisky. I can't say the same about beer, but I never drank much of it. I smoked less than half of the first pack of cigarettes I bought. I threw the rest of them in the hole in the privy behind the bunk house where I slept, when I worked for the potato farmer. The fact that I was shy around girls, no doubt, saved me from sexual sins. That doesn't mean I was innocent in my thought life. Internet wasn't around then. Magazines didn't have such a blatant pornographic content back then. God only knows what I, as an unsaved young man, would have done if I had been exposed to the temptations young men face today.

Now, let's go back to the University of Nebraska and my new friends. The first Wednesday evening my friend, Dean, and Charlie, a friend of his, came to my door and invited me to go with them to a meeting at the Student Union Building. They didn't say what the meeting was about. I didn't ask them, but felt honored to go with them. They led me to an upstairs room where a group of students were gathered. In a few minutes the meeting started. A cordial young man welcomed us to what he called the first Intervarsity meeting of the fall semester. I don't remember what other preliminaries there were before the speaker of the evening was introduced. I don't remember who he was or what he said, but I soon realized that his goal was to convert us to Christianity.

My intellectual pride kicked in, and wouldn't let me believe that anything he said could be true. I said to myself, "I'm not going to be taken in by this." I was impressed, however, by the friendliness of the group. After the meeting several came up to me and introduced themselves, and asked who I was. Several of the girls even came up and introduced themselves, making me feel welcome. After the meeting we went back to our rooms and to our studies.

The agricultural college, where I had most of my classes, was about five miles from the dormitory where I was staying. That meant I had to take a bus from the main campus to the agricultural college campus. In the Lord's plan, Dean was also studying in the agricultural college. He had a car and I often rode with him in the morning. We became better acquainted, since we traveled together.

The next Wednesday evening Dean and Charlie invited me to go with them again to the Intervarsity meeting. In spite of my objections to the purpose of the meeting, I gladly accepted their invitation, because I craved their friendship and enjoyed the social outlet. After a few weeks Dean started having Bible studies once a week in his room, or in the rooms of some of the other students. I started attending those also. Someone gave me a Gideon New Testament. I didn't argue with what was said at the Bible studies, because I valued their friendship. I could see that these young people had something I wanted and needed. I didn't know exactly what it was. Maybe I thought I would absorb it just by being around them. They had joy in their life and a reason for living that I didn't have. Being with them gave me a chance to get acquainted with girls also. I was too shy to make friends with them on my own.

Along about October the students from the Intervarsity group invited me to go with them to a weekend retreat at a camp near Omaha. I took advantage of it and enjoyed it. They had several speakers. I listened without giving any indication that I was accepting or rejecting what I was hearing. Little by little the truth of God was getting through to me, but I was too proud to admit that I was accepting it. The same relationship with them went on throughout the remainder of my first year in college.

My parents didn't have the funds to make it possible for me to stay in the dormitory the next year. To continue my studies I had to make some sacrifices. I borrowed my dad's car and drove to Lincoln to look for a private room where I could stay. Within a day I had found a room near the downtown campus. To pay my expenses I had to look for work. I found a job at the library on the agricultural college campus.

When school started in the fall I looked up my friends. They informed me that the Intervarsity group had planned a picnic at Pioneer Park to start off the New Year. I went with them and renewed my friendship with old friends and made some new ones. More and more I tried to adopt their life style, thinking it would enable me to get what they had. Dean started having a weekly prayer meeting in one of the classrooms at the agricultural college over the noon hour. I joined him and four or five others. After a short time I learned how to pray just like they did; at least I thought I did.

Among the activities the group had planned for the school year was a weekend retreat at a camp in Colorado Springs, Colorado. I went home for the Christmas holiday but went back early to go on that trip to Colorado. There were students there from several other colleges. The main speaker preached from the love chapter, I Corinthians 13. The next big event of the year was a Valentine's banquet. I invited one of the girls to go to the banquet with me. I borrowed Dean's car to go get her and take her home. I thought she might make a good wife for me and wanted to impress her. I began telling her all the things I had done and the big plans I had for my life. I had to stretch the truth in several ways to make it sound more impressive. After the banquet I took her home and went back to my room.

That night, alone in my room, I felt the convicting power of God's Spirit as I had never felt it before. It was as if God was saying, "Russell, you lied to that girl." I knew it was true. I fell on my knees beside my bed and began to weep and pray like I never had before. I called out to God for forgiveness and asked him to save me from my sins. I had heard my Christian friends talk about being saved. I had also heard about being born again and about being a new creature in Christ. I asked for all those things. I later learned that it's all part of the same package. After praying that way I felt a peace come over my soul that I had never felt before. I was a new man. The next morning I took Dean's car back to him. I tried to tell him what happened the night before, but I didn't know how to put it in words. From that night on, I have never had any doubt about my salvation. To God be the glory!

I lost my job at the library, but I soon found another one working for a scientist, who was doing research on chicken eggs. It was my job to wash the utensils he had used during the day. I looked forward to that time when I could think about the exciting new relationship I had with Christ. I have often thought it was a shame that someone hadn't sat down with me to explain the plan of salvation. God knew if I would have been ready before to make that all important decision.

Along with that great victory in my life, also came a great disappointment. I was failing as a college student. In fact, the university sent my parents a letter informing them that I wouldn't be allowed to return to the university, unless I successfully completed several remedial courses. I thought that marked the end of my college career. When I went back home for the summer and found a job working for a rancher. After that I worked again for the aerial spray pilot.

I was a new Christian with a hunger for God. I felt the need of telling my family something about the new relationship I had with Christ. I knew they needed to know about it, but I didn't know how to tell them. One Sunday morning I woke up and decided to go to church. I decided to ask my family at the breakfast table if any of them would like to go with me to church. We all sat down at the table and I began struggling to get the words out of my mouth, but they just wouldn't come. Finally, when everyone was about ready to get up from the table, I asked, "Would anyone like to go with me to church this morning?" They looked at me a bit astonished, but no one said a word. They all got up and went about other things. I got up from the table, changed my clothes, and went to the Methodist Church in Bartlett.

Friend

You too can have a turning point in your life if you haven't. It comes when you recognize that you are a sinner, condemned by God and deserving of his judgment. Then you need to go to God in prayer and ask his forgiveness and the salvation Jesus purchased for you when he died on the cross.

1. "He that believeth on him is not condemned: but he that believeth not is condemned already, because he hath not believed in the name of the only begotten Son of God" (John 3:18).
2. "For all have sinned, and come short of the glory of God" (Romans 3:23).
3. "For if, when we were enemies, we were reconciled to God by the death of his Son, much more, being reconciled, we shall be saved by his life" (Romans 5:10).
4. "For whosoever shall call upon the name of the Lord shall be saved" (Romans 10:13).

The Second Great Turning Point

After I started staying at the motel again I continued going to the Methodist church. After church on Sundays I would go out home for dinner and spend the afternoon there. What I received at the Methodist church didn't satisfy my spiritual hunger. When I went to the pastor he didn't seem to know how to answer my questions. That's why I started looking for Christian programs on the radio. Among the programs I liked to listen to was one called "The Voice of China and Asia" by a man named Bob Hammond. He reported about missionary work in those countries.

During this time two Mormon missionaries came to my motel door and offered to have classes with me. I thought it would be interesting to hear what they had to say. They came in, set up their flannel board, and told their story. They came two or three times. When I asked them questions about the Bible it was obvious that they didn't have much knowledge of it. I told them not to come any more because I didn't agree with what they were teaching. The truth is, I didn't know enough about the Bible to defend myself. Even though I told them not to come back, I rather suspected they would come again the next week. That night I locked my door, turned off the light, and waited for them. Sure enough, they came back. I didn't answer the door. I heard one of them say: "It looks like he ought to be here. His car is here." They left and never came back again.

God used "The Voice of China and Asia" program to speak to my heart about serving him. I kept arguing with God saying, "I could never do that." I reminded God that I had been a failure as a college student. I knew I couldn't serve God without going back to college. Every night I'd listen to that program and argue some more with God. I couldn't convince God that I didn't qualify. He just kept burdening me about it. The truth was that, humanly speaking, I didn't have anything to offer God. I had been a failure. I was struggling with depression. The Bible says in I Corinthians 1:27 that he uses the weak to confound the wise.

One night in October I finally fell on my knees beside my bed and said to God, "I don't have anything to offer. I don't know what I could do, but here's my life. I'm willing to do what ever you want me to do." That was the second turning point in my life.

I had heard some of my Christian friends mention a "Grace Bible Institute" in Omaha. I wrote and asked them if I could come and study there. They sent me information along with papers for reference reports, that they wanted me to have filled out. I asked my friends at the Methodist church to fill them out for me. At first they refused saying I should go to the Wesleyan College at Lincoln. What I had heard about that school didn't leave me with a good impression of it. One of the families at the Methodist church had sent their son there. He came back denying the truths of Christianity. I finally found enough people to fill out the reference reports. I was accepted for the semester beginning in January.

After Christmas I loaded all my earthly belongings into my 1939 Chevy and left early one morning to go to Omaha. I found the institute in an old building on a hill on South 10th Street. Above the entrance of the college were the words: "TO THE PRAISE OF HIS GLORY." I knew I wanted to live to the praise and glory of my Savior. They assigned me to a room where I unloaded my belongings. It was their custom to have a family style meal at the dining hall in the evenings.

I was introduced as a new student and made to feel welcome. I was able to transfer a few of my credits from the University of Nebraska, but for the most part, I was starting out anew as a college student.

I had saved enough money to enroll at the Bible Institute, but in the spring I had to begin working to pay my room and board. I talked to a lady who had an office at the school. Her job was to find work for the students. It wasn't long before I began finding notes in my mail box, telling me about an afternoon job here or there. They were jobs like washing windows or cutting grass.

The Lord did great things for me. Most of my fellow students had grown up in Sunday school and church, and had a knowledge of the Bible that was far superior to mine. In spite of that, at the end of the semester I had passing grades in all my courses. Every student was assigned what was called a "practical work assignment." One month it might be preaching in a street meeting with a team in down town Omaha. The next month it might be helping conduct a service at the rescue mission. With fear and trembling, but trusting the Lord, I entered into those assignments.

When school was out in the spring I went back to Bartlett and spent the summer working for Bob Martin. I looked forward to going back to school in the fall. When the summer was over I added up my assets, and came to the sad reality that I didn't have enough money to return to school. After praying, the Lord seemed to direct me to sell my 1939 Chevy. I sold it and rode to Omaha with a trucker. By taking odd jobs I was able to pay my school bill that year.

The second summer I spent in South Dakota. First I worked for a farmer for a while. Then I took advantage of the opportunity of helping some other students conduct Daily Vacation Bible Schools in rural communities in South Dakota.

I went back to Omaha about two weeks before school started to look for a job. I found work as a night watchman for the school. Later in the fall I worked at a hardware warehouse with some of the other students. It was a better paying job and I was able to buy a car again.

While I was a student at Grace Bible Institute I struggled with the question of church membership. My friends in the Intervarsity group had told me that I would have more influence with people if I wasn't a member of a church. I finally realized that wasn't good advice. I considered joining the church at the college. They baptized by sprinkling. I decided I should study my Bible to see if that was the way to do it. The more I studied, the more convinced I was that baptism should be by immersion. For that reason, I sought out a Baptist church and joined there. It wasn't a real strong Baptist church, but at least, I got baptized biblically.

I was seeking the Lord's will for a wife, but none of the girls at the Bible College appealed to me. Finally, in the third year, I found her. Her name was Margaret Snakenberg. After watching her for a few weeks I finally asked her for a date. The more I came to know her, the more convinced I was that she was the one for me. We enjoyed each other's company. In the spring I was able to visit her parent's farm in Iowa and become acquainted with her family. Our ways parted when summer came.

She went back home to work in her father's business and help at home. I spent the summer working full time at the hardware warehouse. We corresponded by mail. When school started we were able to spend time together again. In October I asked her to marry me. She said yes! Her parents came after her for the Thanksgiving break and I went home with them. I enjoyed talking to her father and helping him with work on the farm. When we returned to Omaha we stopped first at my dorm. Her father got out to unload my luggage. I took the occasion to ask him if I could marry his daughter. By his response, I could tell that he wasn't real excited about it. If I remember right, he said "I suppose it's alright." We planned for a June wedding after we both graduated from Bible College.

**Margaret when she graduated
from High school**

The Long Road To Argentina

The Long Road To Argentina

In the months before our marriage we prayed a lot about the Lord's will for our lives. We both felt called to missions. The big question was "Where should we serve?" Margaret and I studied the globe and prayed about different countries. Every Friday there was a missionary speaker in what was called "Missions Chapel." After a time we noticed that no one had come from Argentina. That made us wonder what was being done there. The more we inquired, the more we felt the Lord leading us there. After we knew where God wanted us to go, he took us down a long road to prepare us.

We applied to a missionary agency. They recommended that I go on for further studies in a seminary. God very definitely intervened in the choice of a seminary. I don't know where we heard of Central Baptist Theological Seminary in Minneapolis, but that's where God led us. At first I had difficulty accepting some of the things they were teaching me, but with time, I saw that my professors could back up what they were teaching from the Bible. Since I couldn't defend my position, I accepted the truth of God's Word

The Lord gave us many blessings while I was in seminary. Our first three children were born. I worked at various jobs, all of which taught me new skills and valuable lessons. God always provided for our needs in amazing ways when my salary wasn't enough. My classes equipped me to do a work for God that I couldn't have done otherwise. It was there also that we made the acquaintance of Wilbur and Dorothy Sanford, veteran missionaries to Argentina. Later they were a tremendous help in getting us into the country and helping us become orientated once we arrived. They are both in their heavenly home now.

After I had graduated from the Bible College I thought I was ready to go to the mission field. However, after graduating from seminary, I realized I still had a lot to learn. I felt I should have some pastoral experience before going to Argentina. I thought it would be better to make my mistakes in the States rather than in Argentina. It proved to be a good decision.

When I graduated from seminary my father-in-law asked me to come and work for him. The Lord hadn't opened the door to any form of Christian service that would, at the same time, enable me to provide for my family. I hadn't spent several years in Bible College and seminary just to be a farm hand, but I needed a job. We loaded all our earthly belongings into a little covered trailer that we bought and moved to Iowa.

We were only in Iowa a short time before some folks from the Calvary Bible Church in North English asked me to preach for them. After a month or two they asked me to be their pastor. It turned into about a three year internship ministry. Not all the experiences I had there were pleasant, but the Lord used all of them to teach me.

During those years we continued to trust the Lord for the provision of our needs. The $50.00 a week that the church gave us was barely enough to pay the rent and cover our basic needs. During the winter months my father in law didn't have much work for me. From week to week we never knew how our needs would be supplied. However we knew that God had promised in his Word that he would supply all our needs (Philipians 4:19) Sometimes people from the church would give us meat from their freezer, or jars of canned food that had been prepared in the summer. Many times they gave us milk and eggs. During the summer we had a large garden.

During my second year of the pastorate we began seeking the Lord's will again about going to Argentina. Maybe it was like putting out a fleece, but I accepted an invitation to candidate at a church in Montana that was seeking a pastor. One cold winter day we boarded a train in Des Moines, Iowa and went to Montana. A short time after we returned home we received a letter from the church. In the letter was a check for us in appreciation for our coming, but along with the check was a letter saying they hadn't called me to be their pastor. We accepted that as a confirmation that God wanted us to make preparations for serving him in Argentina.

I hadn't been ordained. I didn't feel led to seek ordination while I was pastoring the Calvary Bible Church because it was interdenominational. Our membership was still in Faith Baptist Church in St. Paul, Minnesota, where we attended while I was in seminary. I wrote to them and asked if they would ordain me. They responded by saying that we would need to come back up there, so we could acquaint ourselves with the people before they would consider ordination. That meant we needed to drive there on Saturday and come back on Monday. The people were very gracious in giving us a place to stay Saturday and Sunday nights. I had resigned from Calvary Bible Church, so we were free to do that. I was still working for my father-in-law. After about two months of driving to St. Paul every weekend I was ordained.

At that time we were living in an old farm house north of Webster, Iowa. I started working in Washington, Iowa. I drove back and forth to work each day, about 30 miles each way. We started attending Prairie Flower Baptist church not far from Washington, Iowa and moved our membership there. We fell in love with the people there. They were a tremendous blessing to us. We found an old farm house for rent just a mile south of the church. We moved there.

After a number of months we learned that Evangelical Baptist Missions was desirous of starting a work in Argentina. One other couple, Don and Lois Harris, had already applied and been accepted as missionaries to Argentina. After completing all the paper work, we had to make a trip to Patterson, New Jersey to meet with the mission board and be approved. It was the first time we had been in the eastern states. On our way back we enjoyed traveling through the Great Smoky Mountains.

After we were accepted we began the humbling task of setting up a schedule of deputation meetings. Pastors are usually very gracious people, but it's not easy to call them and ask for a place on their church calendar. More often than not they had to say "no." Being repeatedly turned down tempted me to be depressed. I preferred to go on the road and visit pastors personally. I felt I saw more results that way. Little by little, meetings started trickling in. We bought a slide projector and put together a slide presentation with pictures we found here and there to show in the churches where the Lord sent us.

During the summer months I worked at painting houses in and around Washington, Iowa. That worked well because I could take time off for traveling. I took a tape recorder with a Spanish tape in it to work and listened to it over and over again to get familiar with Spanish.

When fall and winter came I couldn't paint houses which caused us to face financial hardships. Thankfully the Lord provided and more meetings started coming in, but we still hadn't gained much support. Our mission board informed us that we had to send all the love offerings we received from the churches to them to build up our outfit and passage fund. I wrote back and boldly told them that they could drop us as missionaries, if need be, but we were going to keep those offerings because we needed them to support our family. They must have understood, because they didn't drop us as missionaries; neither did they say it was alright. They just didn't respond.

We spent nearly three years living by faith while I traveled around the country getting and holding meetings to raise support. Meanwhile, the size of our family was increasing. Margaret had to stay home because we had children in school. Sometimes I was away for two weeks at a time. One time we were thrilled to learn that a doctor's wife had taken on some of our support. It wasn't a great amount, but we were in hopes she would increase it. After our fifth child was born we received a letter from her saying that it appeared that the number of children in our family was increasing faster than the support, and that she wasn't going to continue supporting us. That disappointment meant that we would have to trust the Lord even more to provide for us.

As the third year wore on we still didn't have nearly enough support. Even though the Bible says, "Faithful is he that calleth you, who also will do it," I was getting depressed and thinking we weren't going to make it. I was searching for the best way to throw in the towel with dignity. About that time we had a meeting in a small church in Tipton, Iowa. After the meeting I thought, "These people couldn't help but see that I'm defeated. They won't support us." What a surprise it was to receive a letter from them in less than a week saying they were going to take on some of our support! I was of little faith. God used that to lift my spirits. I wish I would have kept that letter. It was to me what the wagons were to old Jacob when his sons came back from Egypt with an invitation for him to come there to live. (See Genesis 45:27.) I said to myself "It's too soon to quit." Since then, I have had to say that to myself a number of times and keep waiting on God.

God had to bring us to the end of our human resources before he could bless. Support started coming in. Finally we had enough to seriously consider going to language school. We applied and were accepted by the language school at Rio Grande Bible Institute in Edinburg, Texas. There was a truck driver in our church who was regularly making trips to the Rio Grande Valley of Texas to bring back fruit. He let me ride along with him to Edinburg in order that I could look for a house to rent. The first day I was there I found one located beside a school, where three of our children later attended. I took a bus back home the next day.

I made arrangements with an auctioneer I knew to hold an auction sale for us and dispose of a lot of our earthly goods. Most of what we kept was loaded in a U-haul truck. A man from our church offered to drive the truck for us, and we followed in our car on the two day trip from Iowa to southern Texas. We had to stop and stay overnight at a motel. Our children were anxious to get there and see what would be their new home.

We spent nine months there in language school. It was a challenge for us. We went to a Spanish church there for the first time. When we returned to the car after the service, I asked Margaret how many words she recognized. She said "two or three." I hadn't gotten much more than that. We had to cast ourselves again on the grace of God. Philippians 4:13 "I can do all things through Christ which strengtheneth me." When graduation day came we were far from proficient in Spanish, but we had a start.

In the last days of language school I built a shipping crate for the things we had in Texas, that we wanted to take to Argentina. We rented a trailer to haul it to

Our Ministry In Argentina

Our family shortly after arriving in Argentina

Our First Experiences

It was an exciting day when we made our departure for Argentina. We took a cross country bus to New York State, where we participated in the annual conference of our mission board. From there we went on to New York City to fly to Argentina. We arrived in Argentina the next morning; September 13th, 1974. Wilbur Sanford was waiting for us with his Jeep station wagon. We tied our luggage on the top of the Jeep and crawled in to go to his house. When we arrived we were greeted by his wife, Dorothy. She had lunch waiting for us. After lunch they took us to the house that they had rented for us. It was a house that belonged to a family from their church that lived two doors away.

Wilbur gave me some money to use until he could take me to the exchange house to get money changed. He told me to take the bus the next morning to the train station. He said, "I'll be waiting for you at the door of the train station, and we will go on the train to downtown Buenos Aires to the exchange house. I'll introduce you to the people who work there, so you can go on your own the next time."

I got on the bus the next morning. It was standing room only which didn't allow me to see out the windows. I would stoop down every little bit and look between elbows to see if I could see anything that looked like a train station. I consoled myself by thinking "We will cross the tracks when we get to the station. Then I'll know it's time to get off." After going for some time I finally had enough courage to ask a lady if we were near the train station in Martinez. She said, "Oh, we already passed it, but there is another station at the next stop." I got off and thought, "I'll walk back up the tracks the way we came." After walking about two blocks I thought, "I have a lot of money on me. I'm all alone out here. I could easily be robbed. Besides, it may be a long ways to the Martinez station." I went back to where I got off the bus and took a taxi. I thought "By now Wilbur may have given up on me." I told the taxi driver to take me back home. When I arrived, Wilbur and Dorothy were there waiting for me. I explained to them what happened. They were very understanding. Wilbur had something he had to do that afternoon, but Dorothy said she could go with me. She said, "I'll come here to the house to get you and accompany you on the bus." What a relief!

Our first Sunday in Argentina the Sanfords took us to their church. Wilbur asked me to give a testimony. I had a terrible time saying what I wanted to say. I wanted to read a verse of Scripture from Deuteronomy. I said let's go to Deut, Deut, Deut." Someone had to help me say it. I went home from that service defeated. I thought, "After nine months in language school I still can't talk their language." After thinking about it a little I said to myself, "It's too soon to quit."

We were fortunate to be under the tutelage of the Sanfords in our first months in Argentina. They taught us many valuable lessons about Argentine culture. We followed them around to learn all we could from them.

We also went to a summer camp with them and helped in a limited way.

Purchasing Our First House

A few months later we began seeking the leading of the Lord as to where we should start our first church. Once I took a three hour train trip to the city of Rosario and spent two nights in a hotel there. I don't know why, but I didn't feel the Lord was leading us there. After that I often spent two or three days a week going to different neighborhoods in the suburbs of Buenos Aires, and spent the day walking around. I must have worn out a pair of shoes in those months walking neighborhoods. More and more I felt the Lord was leading us to the county of Matanza. It's one of the most heavily populated areas of Greater Buenos Aires. San Justo is the biggest commercial center. I walked the streets in neighborhoods beyond San Justo. Some days I walked in Ciudad Evita. Other days I spent in Casanova and Laferrere. More and more I felt led to the city of Laferrere, which was a fast growing residential area.

After feeling peace about starting in Laferrere I started going to real estate agencies to ask about houses that were available. An optometrist in our home church offered to loan us money to buy a house. One day Wilbur Sanford brought Margaret, the children, and myself to Laferrere to look at a house I thought might work for us. We wanted his advice. We were especially led to one particular house because two different real estate agents had brought me to see it. When the second real estate agent stopped in front of it, I said to him, "I've already seen this house." It was the one we finally bought. It was what is called a chalet on Santa Rosa Street. It had a big back yard where our children could play, and was only two blocks from a bus stop.

It takes several weeks to do all the paper work to buy a house in Argentina. We were glad for Wilbur Sanford's supervision. The day finally came when we were given the keys and it was ours. It was the first house I ever owned. During the previous weeks Margaret had been packing up our things for the move. Fortunately we didn't have a lot of material possessions. The barrels and crates we had shipped to Argentina had arrived previous to our buying the house. Early one morning the moving van arrived, and we loaded our earthly belongings. The moving van driver reluctantly agreed to take our family in the truck. Three of the boys were shut in the dark in the back of the truck. By noon we had everything unloaded in our new home, and we were left with the task of putting everything in its place.

Starting Our First Church

Since we planned to start a church in our neighborhood, we felt the need of getting acquainted with our neighbors. Our children made friends right away, but it wasn't all that easy for Margaret and I.

Some time later we learned that our neighbors talked among themselves and asked, "What are we going to do? They are evangelicals. They are North Americans. They don't speak our language." With time they learned that we could speak their language even though it wasn't fluently.

We didn't start having meetings until we had been in the neighborhood for about six months. I made a wooden sign and put it in front of our house to let people know that we had a church at our house. Since we had five children we already had a little congregation to start with. We set up all the chairs in the house in our large room in the back where we had church. Our children went out and invited neighbor children. There were always some in the service. Getting adults to come was more difficult.

The Lord's mercies never fail. He knew we needed help. Lamentations 3:22-23 says "It is of the Lord's mercies that we are not consumed, because his compassions fail not. They are new every morning; great is thy faithfulness." One day two teenage boys from Uruguay appeared at our door. They asked if they could stay at our house and look for work in our neighborhood. We took them in since a missionary we knew in Uruguay had given them our name and address. They were a tremendous help to us with the language. They were instrumental in getting adults and teenagers to come to church. One afternoon some children were throwing rocks into our back yard. I stepped up on a box that enabled me to see over the wall, and rebuke them. Just then a rock hit me in the forehead. I recognized the boy who threw the rock. The Uruguayan fellows went with me to the boy's house, which was about three blocks away. I didn't take time to dress the wound. Blood was running down my face and dripping off my chin. Some of the neighbor children joined us, which must have made an interesting procession as we went up the street. The boy wasn't home when we arrived at his house, but his father was there. We told him what happened. He promised to punish his son. He also took me to the pump behind his house and washed my face in cold water. As we made our way back home, we met the boy who threw the rock. The Uruaguayan fellows threatened to give him a good beating if they ever found him around our house. He made himself scarce for a long time after that.

I started going door to door in the neighborhood passing out tracts and inviting people to come to our church. More often than not, people asked, "What did you say?" When I finally got across to them that we were there to start a church they said, "We don't need a church here. We already have one." They, of course, referred to the Catholic Church. They knew where the church was, but most of them seldom, if ever, went to mass. After hearing the same refrain over and over again, I started getting discouraged. I asked myself, "What are you doing here? You can't make yourself understood. People don't want what you have to offer." The thought of admitting defeat and going back to the States was an awful tempting option. I had to sit myself down and have a serious talk with myself. I said, "Russell, you didn't spend nearly three years running around the country raising support, so you could come here to quit. You didn't spend nine months in Texas studying Spanish, so you could come here and quit. Haven't you been telling people the last three or four years that God called you to be a missionary in Argentina?" I had to admit that quitting wasn't an option. I'm glad God didn't let me quit.

Many children and young people have been in our churches over the years. Several made a profession of salvation. We still have contact with a few of those that were led to the Lord back in those early days. Two of them are now a husband and wife team, and are active in serving the Lord. I had a part in their wedding.

Sometimes, as I worked around the yard, it was a thrill to hear neighbor children singing choruses that they had learned in church. One time, for some reason, a harmonica fell into my hands. I don't know the first thing about playing a harmonica, but I could blow on it and make noise. I took it out to the front gate, and called some of the neighbor children over who were playing across the street. I showed them the harmonica and asked if they would like to sing some gospel songs accompanied by the harmonica. They were all excited about it. I suggested some songs I knew they had learned by memory. I said, "Let's sing 'Jesus Loves Me'." They all sang the song while I blew on the harmonica. They didn't know I didn't really know how to play it. We had a lot of fun with it.

For the first year or more we were without transportation of our own. Wilbur Sanford bought a better vehicle and sold us the Jeep wagon that he drove to the airport to pick us up the day we arrived. Having a car meant I needed to get a driver's license. With fear and trembling I drove to the driver's license examining station. I didn't pass the test because I couldn't understand well enough what the examiner was asking me to do. He said I could come back a week later and try again. That time I passed because I understood what I was supposed to do.

Having a car was an asset to our ministry. It meant we could join the Sanfords in activities they planned. Before that we would take our church for a picnic in a wooded area about two miles away. We loaded the food and athletic equipment in a wheelbarrow and walked there and back. In the summer months the Sanfords reserved a private recreation area near the town of Pilar. That was about a 30 mile trip for us. There was a swimming pool, playground equipment, and lots of grass and shade trees. After the noon meal we gathered for a time of singing and a Bible lesson.

One day we were on our way to Pilar with a number of neighborhood children. We were on a busy six lane highway when an axle broke on the old Jeep wagon. The car slid to a stop, but the tire went careening on ahead of us. Brakes were squealing as cars slowed down and went around us. I got everyone out of the jeep and they waited along side of the highway while I went on ahead to retrieve the tire. We stood there for a while praying and asking ourselves, "What do we do now?" After a while a man, driving a tow truck, stopped and asked if we needed help. He was a God send. He took us and the car to a garage where the axle was replaced.

By the time that was done it was too late to go on to Pilar, and we returned home.

Before going to Argentina I had read books and taken courses in "missionary principles and practice." I'm sure it was a help to me, but it certainly didn't give advice as to what I was to do in situations in which I was to find myself. There were questions like how to rescue the neighbor's dog when it gets caught under the fence, just when it was time to start a worship service. I wasn't told how to climb a tree, and rescue a cat hanging upside down in the V of two branches. It didn't tell me how to use my old jeep wagon as an ambulance and take people to the hospital in an emergency. Being involved in those things helped us get acquainted with our neighbors and endear ourselves to them.

Our Children's Education

We enrolled our children in a Christian school in a Baptist church in San Justo that was about eight miles away. We paid a neighbor girl to take them on the city bus each day and go back after them. Argentine schools are only in session for half a day. One morning I had to take them to school. We got to the end of our block when a neighbor met us. He said, "There isn't any school today. There has been a revolution." We went back home and turned on the radio. He was right. The military had taken over the country. We lived under a military government for some time after that.

After a year of having our children in the Christian school we began to realize that the school's standards were not our standards. They were going to teach them how to dance and expose them to questionable movies. We thought, "It's not worth the sacrifice, if they are exposed to the same temptations they are exposed to in the public schools. The next year we enrolled them in a private school in Casanova. The following year we decided to home school them. Most of the responsibility fell on Margaret because I felt that I needed my time to invest in the ministry. The fact that all of them either graduated from college or, at least, had some college training, attests to the fact that their home school education was not a detriment to them.

Police Protection

We went through some exciting times after Argentina went to war in 1982 in an attempt to reclaim the Falcon Islands from England. The war lasted for 74 days. The police arrived at our house just a few hours after we heard that war had broken out. They asked to see our documents and said they were sent for our protection. I thought it meant that we were under house arrest. I told them I had somewhere to go that morning. They said," You go ahead and do whatever you need to do. We aren't going to hinder you." They stayed at our door day and night until about three weeks after the war was over. Some of our fellow missionaries became nervous and went back to the States during the war. We said, "We don't have anything to worry about. God sent police here to take care of us." We were the only missionaries we heard of that had police protection during the war. "For thou hast been a shelter for me, and a strong tower from the enemy." says Psalm 61:3. We never knew for sure why the police came. Perhaps it was because some of the children in the neighborhood called us "the Englishes" because we spoke English.

We had some interesting experiences with the police. We had a chance to witness to most of them. Sometimes one of them would come into our service while the other one stayed out front. During the day they would come in to use the bathroom. We started noticing that every time one of them came out of the bathroom, he had a strong smell of an after shave lotion that I had in there. Many times our boys would set up a little table in front of our house and play a game of checkers with them. Sometimes we gave them mate (an Argentine tea that nearly everyone there drinks).

One morning, when I went out to greet the police, I noticed there was a pile of copper tubing and electrical wire on the drive way in front of our car. I asked them where they got it. They said they found some thieves during the night. When they attempted to apprehend them, they dropped the stolen goods and ran. They brought the goods to our driveway. They asked me if I knew where the thieves might have stolen those things. I thought of a place where some men were building a house. I went over there and asked them if someone had broken in and stolen things during the night. They said "yes." I asked them what had been stolen. When they told me it was electrical wire and copper tubing, I said, "I think I know where it is," and brought them to the house. After the police questioned them they let them come in and get the goods that had been stolen. One policeman said I was a good detective.

One day I knew that one of the policemen had spent most of the day at the house of one of his friend's about a block away. When I came home in the afternoon the policeman was back, but he was drunk. He wanted to treat us to a barbeque that night. I tried to talk him out of it, but he insisted that I take him in the car to get some meat. I didn't want to do it, but I didn't think it wise to argue with a drunken policeman, who was carrying a gun. We went to a meat market where he got some meat. I later learned that he walked out without paying for it. Then he decided he needed to go to his house to get some medicine he was taking. He insisted that I take him there. As we were driving down the highway, he saw a car going down the road without lights. He said, "Hey, we gotta stop that car," so we pulled him over and the policeman got out and rebuked him. When he came back he said, "I should have taken him to the police department, but I couldn't do that because you are with me." When we returned to our house I was able to persuade him to return to his friend's house, where he had been drinking to make his barbeque. I'm sure we wouldn't have enjoyed having a barbeque with a drunken policeman.

During the war the Pope came to visit Argentina. Most of the police force was occupied in protecting the Pope. They left one elderly policeman by himself at our house for nearly 24 hours. I went to the police department and asked if they couldn't leave us without police protection for a while, so he could be relieved. About an hour later they sent two other policemen.

Some weeks after the war ended I was out visiting door to door and happened to come to the door of that elderly policeman, who had spent 24 hours at our house. He was thrilled to see me, and wanted to ask my advice about something. Since I was a "reverend" he thought I could give him some good advice. He started telling a story about how a teenage girl had come to his window at night, and said she was in love with him. He let her in and they had sexual relations. The question he had for me was "Wouldn't it be alright to take her in as my common law wife?" I jokingly said, "Look, it isn't going to be very long until that girl realizes that you can't dance like the younger men can and she is going to dump you like a rotten potato." Then I gave him some advice about biblical purity. I don't know if he took my advice. I never saw him again.

Neighborhood Projects

In both neighborhoods where we started churches, the Lord gave us an occasion to work with the neighbors in solving a problem. The first problem was a drainage ditch that was full of weeds and trash. Every time it rained hard the water would back up and flood some of the houses. Ours was one of them. We petitioned the municipality to do something about it. We went around and got the neighbors to sign a petition. After several months they finally sent a dredge and truck to clean out the ditch. Along with several of the neighbors, we took sandwiches and something to drink at noon to the men who were working.

In the second neighborhood a problem arose when the municipality paved several streets. Ours was one of them. They did it just before an election so everyone would be inclined to vote them back in again. After the election, however, they started sending us a bill for it. We had reason for saying, "Hey, we didn't ask for this. There is no reason why we should pay for it." We learned that the municipality had done the same thing in other neighborhoods. Our church served as a meeting place for what we called "street meetings." Neighbors signed petitions which we took to the municipality. They still insisted that we had to pay. Plans were then made to go to the state capital and protest. One day a caravan of about thirty bus loads of us went to the state capital and made a big demonstration in front of one of the office buildings. We closed off the street. Some beat on drums while we all shouted in unison, "We aren't going to pay." They invited some of our leaders to go inside and talk to the officials. About ten days later we received a letter in the mail saying we wouldn't have to pay for the pavement.

The Growth Of Our First Church

Little by little our first church grew. We started reaching more adults. Among those who were saved were Juan Carlos and his wife, Milka. She came first and received assurance of her salvation. Juan Carlos gave all appearance of being one of those men who couldn't be reached with the gospel. One day Milka came and asked me to go to where Juan Carlos worked, and let him know that she received word that a relative of his had died in Uruguay. I found him and brought him back home. That gave me a chance to get next to him. Some weeks after that, they were separated for a time. Milka suffered what could be called a nervous breakdown. Margaret prayed with her every day for nearly two months. Margaret and I, and another lady from the church, went to where Juan Carlos was staying and brought him home. The next day I had a talk with him, and persuaded him that he should stay home and take care of his family.

A few weeks later we had evangelistic meeting in a big tent in our back yard. We invited our fellow missionary, Don Harris, to come up from Mar del Plata to preach for us. We showed an evangelistic film each night before the preaching. To get Juan Carlos there, I told him we needed some one to run the movie projector. I knew how to do it, but asking him to do it proved to be a way to get him there. He sat through the preaching each night, but made no decision. Shortly after that, Don Harris and his wife came to our house for a visit. We invited Juan Carlos and Milka to come too. While the ladies were praying in the other room, Don talked to Juan Carlos about his need of accepting Christ as his Savior. He said he was ready, and Don led him to the Lord. Then we called the ladies. Don said to Milka, "Juan Carlos has something to tell you." It was an emotional moment, when he told her that he had accepted Christ as his Savior. They embraced and we all shed tears of joy.

Our church grew to the point that we knew we needed a bigger meeting place. We had saved money from the offerings and had some in a savings account. It wasn't nearly enough to buy a property. I put a Bible verse on the wall in front of the room where we were meeting that said, "With God all things are possible." We began looking for property for sale and found a store building with an attached apartment about four blocks away. The only draw back was that it was on a dirt street, and it was hard to get there with the car after a rain. Never-the-less, by putting some money with what the church had saved up; we were able to buy the property. We agreed to let Juan Carlos and Milka live in the apartment. Little by little the church paid us what we loaned them. We worked for several weeks renovating the building. Several years later, the Lord answered prayer in that the street in front of the church was paved.

Our first church building in Argentina

Some weeks after we started having services there, Juan Carlos told me that he felt God was calling him to preach. I was thrilled about that. I began teaching him all I could. He took some seminary classes, but finally gave it up because it was too much of a sacrifice going to seminary for three hours at night after working all day. After we had invested fifteen years in the church, we installed him as pastor and began seeking the Lord's will about starting another church.

Short Wave Radio

In 1987 I became interested in short wave radio. Some of our children were studying in the States. Apart from letter writing, we didn't have any way to communicate with them. We didn't even have a telephone. Jimmy Strickland, one of the Bible Baptist missionaries, was a short wave radio operator. He explained to me what I had to do to get started.

While we were in the Sates for a furlough I dedicated all my spare time to studying in hopes of being able to pass the test to get a license to be a short wave radio operator. The biggest challenge was the test on the Morse code. When I took the test, I failed the Morse code part, but they gave me a novice license. That left me very limited as to the bands I could use as a short wave radio operator. I felt defeated. Never-the-less, when we returned to Argentina, I went to the government officials and asked for a license. I was told they would give me a license equivalent to the license I had in the States. To my surprise, and to the praise of God, they gave me a license that gave me full privileges. I bought a used short wave radio from Jimmy Strickland, who came and helped me put up an antenna on a tower that Juan Carlos had made and set up for me. I started operating on what was called the "halo band." That was the band the missionaries used to communicate with relatives and friends in the States. It was an exhilarating experience to be able to communicate with people all the way from the southern tip of Argentina to Canada. After internet came into widespread use, I discontinued using the radio. Internet was more dependable

The Second Church

We put our house up for sale with faith that by the time it sold we would know the Lord's leading about where we were to go next. I spent several days each week riding my motor scooter around looking at neighborhoods. I went to real estate agencies and they took me to look at properties they had for sale. One day a real estate agent took me to look at a building in a neighborhood that I had never entered. It was a store front with living quarters in the back and upstairs. A few days later I took Margaret and some friends from the church to look at it. They all thought it would be a good location. Several times I went on my motor scooter and looked around the neighborhood. I wanted to see if there were other churches near by, but I didn't find any.

The building where our second church meets

Our house hadn't sold yet so we were limited as to the amount of money we could offer for it. We made an offer that, at the time, would have been a little over $7000.00. It was considerably less than what they were asking for it. We didn't have much hopes of getting it at that price. The next day the real estate man was at our door with the good news that the seller had accepted our offer. He told us that the seller had put the house up as collateral for a loan, and he was going to lose it to the bank if he didn't pay off the loan within a short time. We began praying fervently that our house would sell, and God answered within a few weeks. With the money we were paid from the sale of the house, we were able, not only to buy the new property, but make a number of improvements on it.

From day one, starting a second church in Laferrere was a challenge for us. We called it "Calvary Baptist Church." We were in what is called "Union village." We started with children and gained some young people after a time. Our children were a tremendous help in recruiting other children and young people. Reaching adults in Union Village was a struggle. By that time I had a better command of the Spanish language. I could talk to adults, and many were willing to listen, but no one seemed to take much interest in spiritual things. We had good success with children, and almost from the start we had youth meetings on Saturday nights.

In Union Village we continued using a little paper I started putting out while we were at the first church. The title was "Light In The Way." It was small enough that two of them could be printed on both sides of a legal size sheet of paper. We usually had 2000 of them printed each time. I wrote an evangelistic article that was printed in it. Having a computer greatly facilitated setting it up. As I walked down the street I would roll them up and stick them in the gates in front of the houses. As a result of this effort, the first adults began attending our church. They weren't faithful and didn't contribute much to the church, but for several years now there have been relatives of that family in the church. The "Light in the Way" papers served to inform people about our church and let them know where we were located.

About five years after we moved to Union Village we started a radio ministry entitled "The Baptist Hour." It was a half hour program with music interspersed between preaching and announcements. Thankfully we gained a good family in the church as a result of the radio program. After about two years I gave up the radio ministry, because we weren't seeing enough results from it to justify the time I was spending on it.

About two weeks after the first family came as a result of the radio program, someone told me about a family that was interested in coming to our church. We went to visit them and they started coming. What a thrill it was to have two families in our church within the space of about three weeks. We had gone for years with only children, young people, and occasionally a few women. It was a thrill to me to hear a man say, "Pastor, what can I do to help?"

The truth of the matter is, before those two families started attending, we had begun thinking about giving up on getting a church established in Union Village. We had spent several weeks going one or two days each week to another city, where we went door to door talking to people. The name of the city was Ponteveedra. The people living there were higher class. They received us well, but we saw little fruit from our labors. We looked for a meeting place there, but didn't find anything we could afford to rent. We gave up on that work after the two families started attending the church in Union Village.

The Third Church

In 1999 we went back to the States for a furlough. We were praying about the possibility of starting yet another church. We didn't know how it would be possible. We returned to Argentina in January of 2000. Some weeks later we went to "Hope Village" to visit a family that had been in our church for a time several years before. They were a family of ten children. The mother of the family, Celia, was a sister of a lady who had come to our church as a result of the "Light in the Way" papers we had passed out. After being in our church for a short time, the family moved to another neighborhood about five kilometers away. For some time we went to their house on Sunday afternoons to have a discipleship class with them. Sometimes I went there on Sunday morning to bring them to Sunday school and church. The father, Pablo, made a profession of salvation, but hadn't shown much Christian growth. They had a little grocery store in their house, and he stayed home Sunday morning to run the store. Later they moved to "Hope Village" where we went to visit them. The mother suggested that maybe we could start a church in their neighborhood. We gave it some thought, but it still looked like it was outside the realm of possibility.

Several times after that we went to visit the family. Celia not only suggested that we start a church there, but pled with us to do so. The church in Union Village wasn't strong enough that we could take anyone from it to start another church. I felt like all my time was needed there. However, after some time of praying, I felt the Lord was saying, "It's time to go out to Hope Village and start a work there." Since it was in "Hope Village" the logical name for the church would be "Hope Baptist Church."

At first we started having a weekly discipleship class with Pablo and his family of ten children. We invited their neighbors to join us and some started coming. Then we began looking for a meeting place. After a few weeks we found a little store front, about the size of a one car garage, which we rented. Pablo was a good carpenter. He made a pulpit and some benches for us. We started having services on Sunday afternoon. At first the congregation consisted mainly of his family and ours.

After a few weeks we hung a sign in front of the building to let people know that we had a Baptist church there. Shortly after we put up the sign we were visited by a young couple and their little boy. After the service he told me that they had been attending a Southern Baptist Church, but had left in disgust because the church had gone charismatic. He knew of several other families who had left for the same reason. They continued attending our church for a few weeks. Then they started visiting the other families, who had left the Southern Baptist Church and several started attending our church. Through the ministry of the church some neighbors were also saved and they too started attending our church. It wasn't long before our little store front was crowded out.

We went on for about a year that way. Sometimes we had people standing in front because there wasn't room inside for more. Some of those who came already had experience as Sunday school teachers. We had a very small room in the back that we used for a class room when they couldn't meet outside. We also had a children's class in our van out in the street. During the worship service the nursery was also in the van.

The Lord, through unusual circumstances, provided for our need of a property. One day we heard that one of the families attending our church had a special need. We stopped at their house and learned of the trial they were going through. Their oldest son had been running with the wrong crowd. One of the boys he was with had shot a taxi driver. When that happened the boys all ran and hid. When friends of the dead taxi driver heard what had happened, they went out looking for the boys. By the grace of God, the son of the family in our church escaped, but they did find the boy who killed the taxi driver and killed him. The family from our church feared that the angry mob might come looking for their son also. For the boy's protection, and the well being of the family, we took the boy to stay at our house for a few days.

The family quickly made arrangements to move to another province. Before they left they offered to sell their house to our church for $10,000.00. That was a good price for the property since it was only three blocks from the commercial center. It was also on a boulevard that is one of the main entrances to the commercial center. We were able to get a loan for $10,000 and the church agreed to pay off the loan by designating half of each month's offerings toward making the payments.

The house on the property was just a little prefab wooden shack on the back of the lot. As soon as we took possession we moved our church to the house. It didn't give us much more room than we had before, but we made do. We put up the church sign at the new property which attracted a few more Christians, who were looking for a good church. We prayed that the Lord would show us what to do next.

During this time Argentina was going through some serious economic trials. All the men in the church were without work. Little came in when we took up the offerings. Bartering centers were set up in every community. People traded what they could live without in exchange for food, clothing and basic necessities. We often went to a wholesale market and bought fruits and vegetables to give to the people on Sundays.

It was obvious that, under the circumstances, the people would never be able to build a building. For that reason, I made the need known among our supporting churches and individuals. Doing so went against my convictions, because I was of the opinion that a church should build its own building, but the Lord gave me peace about it. To our surprise, money started coming in to build a building. It was also at a time when the exchange for the U. S. dollar was in our favor. When it became obvious that money was going to come in for the building, we called the people together and began making plans to build. After several sessions we agreed on a tentative floor plan. One of the ladies in the church gave me the name of an architect that she knew. I called him and made arrangements for him to meet me at the church. A few days after I talked to him and explained to him what we had in mind, he had it all drawn out, complete with trees in front of the building. I had never been involved in a building project and had a lot to learn. The men in the church told me that the first step was to hire a contractor to lay the footings and put up the columns. We planned for a two story building.

From the beginning it was my desire that the men in the church be involved in the building project. That way they would feel it was their building. Besides, they needed work. It was difficult to find a contractor willing to take on the project, if he had to hire the men of the church. Contractors already had men working for them. We finally found one. I told him "If any of my men aren't doing their job, you can fire them."

It was an exciting day when the men started digging holes for the footings. To me, they were massive holes which were dug for each column. When they were all dug and filled with cement, the men started putting up forms for the columns. Some of the men were busy making steel frames out of rods to put in the center of the forms for the columns. It must have taken them nearly six weeks to put up all the forms and fill them with cement. When the cement was set enough they took the boards down and used them to build the forms for the cross beams to support the second floor.

Something that surprised me was that the architect was there working every day along side the other men. I was paying him to be the architect, but I felt compelled to pay him as a day laborer also.

When the cement was set in the cross beams, plans were laid for pouring the second floor. I had seen work teams pouring cement for a second or third floor, but I had never seen it done first hand. The architect hired a man to come in who had the equipment needed to lift the cement to the second floor. It consisted of a winch and cable mechanism that lifted a large bucket from street level to the second floor. The bucket held a cement mixer of cement at a time. A big crew of men was needed to do the job. Several worked at street level mixing cement and pouring it into the bucket. If I remember right, they had two cement mixers working at the same time. Other men worked above with wheel borrows, taking the cement from the bucket and pouring it on the floor. Some worked at spreading and smoothing it. Men came from other churches to help us that day. We provided a barbecue dinner for them. After the cement hardened on the second floor, the men started putting up the forms for the columns for the walls of the second floor.

When the columns were all up for the second floor, the project took a giant step forward because Margaret's brother, Lyle Snakenberg, came from the States with a team of ten workers. We made arrangements for them to stay at a camp a few miles further away. They stayed for 10 days and put the roof on the building, as well as laying the bricks for some of the outside walls. Before they left, they offered to leave us a number of the tools that they brought with them. I debated about how to distribute them evenly. Some were power tools, and others were just hand tools. We decided to sell them at auction to the men who were working on the building. The last afternoon the team was there we had an auction sale. I was the auctioneer. The men didn't have much money. They were happy with the tools they bought at a cheap price. The money that came in was used for the expenses of building materials.

The next few months the men from the church finished laying up the brick for the walls and pouring the first floor. Paul, who I mentioned earlier, made the doors for the outside and inside entrances. All this time we continued meeting in the little prefab house in the back. People had to walk around or over piles of sand and crushed rock to get in, but they didn't mind. They were all excited about the changes they saw in the building each week. Long before the new church building was completed we started meeting in the new building. The old pre-fab house out back was torn down, and given to one of the men in the church to make some improvements on his house.

As soon as the basic necessities for the building were completed the funds stopped coming. Small improvements continued to be made as the Lord provided. An apartment upstairs has never been finished.

Our third church when the building was completed

From the time we started Hope Baptist Church until we went home on furlough in 2011, I tried to carry the load of pastoring two churches. It was more than strength and time allowed. I had some relief because we spent the winter months in the States. In March of 2011 we installed Marcelo Avelar as pastor. He is man who was a member of the church and assumed more and more of a leadership role.

The Search For Leaders

My dream, as a missionary, has always been that of starting a church and leaving it in the hands of a qualified national pastor, so I could go out and start another church. We did that with our first church. Before we came back to the States for a furlough in 2006, we left a man in charge of Calvary Baptist Church. He had great ideas and we had hopes that he would be able to stay on as pastor. When we returned to Argentina, the church had grown and we were encouraged. It wasn't long, however, before we realized that we weren't in agreement with some things he was doing. Others in the church also began to question his leadership. When I tried to correct him, he wasn't humble enough to accept it. For some months, we tried to come to an agreement. We finally saw that it wasn't going to work and were relieved when he resigned.

In August of 2007 we came back for a six week sabbatical. In our absence we left a young man in the church in charge of the preaching under the supervision of the deacon. After we returned we had hopes we could train him as a future pastor. More and more we realized that he wasn't willing to accept correction.

At Calvary Baptist church in Laferrere Freddy Paz is presently serving as pastor. He is a young man from Peru He had seminary training in Peru. He has a wife and two children. The church is going good under his leadership.

Surprise Surprise!

The architect that I mentioned that we hired to draw the plans for Hope Baptist church is a man by the name of Javier Callisaya. His parents are from Bolivia, but he and all his brothers and sisters were born in Argentina. He started attending our church during the construction project. After about two months of being in church, he was at a youth activity we had at the home of one of the families. I approached him and asked him if he didn't think he should be saved. He agreed, so I took him out to our van and explained the plan of salvation to him. He humbly accepted the Lord as his Savior. Shortly after that he began showing an interest in our daughter, Priscila, who was born in Argentina. Their relationship continued to deepen until they were married in the spring of 2005.

Some Interesting Experiences

The Trials And Triumphs
Of Buying A Van In Argentina

It's 4:45 in the afternoon. I look inside the coffee shop where I agreed to meet my lawyer at 5:00 in the afternoon. He is nowhere to be seen. I wait outside for him. I feel a little nervous standing on the street with so many people passing by. I hope no policeman is watching and wondering why I'm loitering around here. At almost 5:00 my lawyer arrives. He and I are going to see what we can do about getting the money back that I have invested in a loam company in hopes of getting a loan to buy a new van.

It all started in November. A loan company promised to give me 50,000 Australes to buy a new van. (Argentine money was called Australes then.) It was later changed back to pesos) My responsibility was to make 10 payments in advance and then we would get the money. After that there would be 21 more fixed monthly payments. They said we would receive the money in two months if not sooner. We had hopes of buying the van by the end of December. I talked to several dealers. Two dealers offered to sell me the van we wanted if we could get the money no later than the 10th of January. After making the eleventh payment I talked to the loan company and they assured me that there would be no problem with getting the money before the 10th of January if I would make another payment. I made that payment, but when it came time for them to give me the money the man I talked to lied to me and, more than once, failed to show up for a scheduled appointment. Once he said, "You come to the office at 4:00 tomorrow and I'll be there with the check." He didn't show. The loan company gave me a number where he could be reached, but when I got him on the phone he had an excuse for not coming. He said he would have the money next week. I told him that would be too late. He said, "Don't worry. I'll talk to the dealer and fix it up" and he hung up. The next week went by and nothing happened. I went to the downtown office and they said, "Any day now it should be coming." They assured me I would be getting a letter in the mail to notify me that the check was ready. After waiting for a week for the letter we began to suspect that we had been taken in by a scam. A close friend from the church went with me to see a lawyer we knew. He said, "If nothing happens by the end of March let me know and I'll see what I can do." When the end of March came we took the contract to him and he said he would look into it. He called back a few days later, and said he turned it over to another lawyer who was more knowledgeable in such cases. He told us that we should go to that lawyer's home to see him that evening. When we arrived, he turned out to be a prototype of Sherlock Holmes. He was blind in one eye and smoked a pipe almost continually. He said it would cost us 500 Australes for him to make a study of the case and tell us what he could do about it. We employed him, and he told us to come back in a week. When we went back he told us in a nice way that I was a fool for having signed a contract like that. He said, "It's a legal scam." He didn't give us much hope that he could be of any help. We had been praying about it. We had already decided that the best we could do was to attempt to retrieve the money that we had invested. It would be at a loss because inflation of 10-15% a month meant that it had been losing that much value each month. The lawyer said, "Why don't you go in and talk to them, and see what they say about giving your money back? If they agree to give it back right away you could save the 3000 Australes I would have to charge you."

That sounded like good advice and the next time I went down town, I mustered up all the courage I had and went in to demand my money back. The first man I talked to said, "Wait a minute. If you want your money back you'll have to go talk to someone else." He gave me a calling card and sent me down the street a half a block. It was a big office building with an assortment of buttons to press for the floor and office you wanted. I pressed the corresponding button and a voice responded saying, "What do you want?" I said, "I came to see about getting my credit money back." The door buzzed to let me in and I took the elevator to the 4th floor. I had to wait awhile and then was ushered into a room where a woman was seated behind a big desk. She invited me to have a seat and asked me what I wanted. I showed her my contract and told her I wanted my money back. She looked at it briefly and said, "But you would be better off to continue making payments." I said, "No, I've made all the payments I'm going to make, because the loan company isn't completing their part of the deal." She said, "Yes, you can get your money back, but you will have to wait 90 days and the loan company will discount something for all the payments you made at the bank." I said, "You mean I have to wait 90 days?" She said, "That's right." I said, "That doesn't sound right. I keep losing money all the time because of inflation." She opened her desk drawer and pulled out a slip of paper and said, "If you want your money back, I'll give you a date when you can get it back." I said, "I'd like to study it a little more first." I started to ask her another question, but she interrupted me and said, "I told you, if you want it back I'll give you a date when you can get it. If not, take your contract and go." I could see I wasn't going to get anywhere talking to her. I took my contract and left.

We went back to tell the lawyer what I found out. He said, "If you would like, I'll go with you and talk to her." He told me I wouldn't have to pay him anything for doing that. I thought, "Why not? I don't have anything to lose." That's why I was waiting for him that day at the coffee shop across the street from the loan company office.

When he arrived we sat down to a cup of coffee, while we discussed what strategy would be best to take. I had already given a lot of thought to what arguments we might use to persuade the loan company to do something. I presented to the lawyer what I thought might move them. I said, "We plan to buy this van, not for our personal use, but for the church. We work in a poor neighborhood and a lot of people can't afford to go to church on the bus. We plan to use this van to pick them up and bring them to church. It's very possible that the van would also be used as an ambulance, since most people where we live don't have a car and they often call on me to take them to the hospital in an emergency." The lawyer listened attentively to my plan.

He asked if I had anything to prove that I was a pastor. In God's providence we were making application to have meetings at the house where we lived. Since I'm the president of our mission organization in Argentina, the government informed me that I needed a paper that shows I'm the president, and that the headquarters of our mission was at our house. That very day I had been to the office of the Minister of Religion and Culture, and they had given me that impressive looking paper. I pulled it out of my briefcase and handed it to the lawyer.

He said, "I think we can do something with this." I could see the think wheels turning for a little while, and then he said, "How would it be if we say that the money for the van has been entrusted to you, and now you will need to file an affidavit with the Minister of Religion and Culture saying that you lost the money because you were the victim of a scam? In the affidavit, of course, the loan company will have to be mentioned as the cause of the loss." He thought that the loan company wouldn't want to be implicated in a scam. I agreed that it sounded worth trying.

We went down the street to talk to the woman behind the big desk. When we arrived she invited us in. I thought, "It's going to be interesting to see her tangle with a lawyer. She slapped a little guy like me down in a hurry. I'll bet she doesn't do that to the lawyer." I introduced him to her and let him take over. He presented his argument to her and asked what would hinder them from giving my money back. It was almost amusing to see the sweet spirit she had with him. You would never have known it was the same woman. He asked her how long it would take to get the money. She said more than once, "It won't take long." She asked him to come back the next day and talk to the agency's' lawyer. They agreed on a time for the meeting and we left. When we got down to the street he said, "You call me tomorrow night and I'll let you know how it went."

The next night I called him and he said, "I think we are making progress." He wanted me to come to his office to talk to him. My friend and I went on Thursday evening to talk to him. He said the loan company had promised to give us the money if I would make another payment. I said, "Wait a minute. That sounds like more of what we have heard all along." He said, "No, let me explain. I realized that so I talked to them about it. They promised to give you a signed statement saying you would get the money in 10 days if you make another payment." I said, "The only way I'll do that is if we can go to the man's office and get him to promise to give me that signed statement immediately after we make the payment." He agreed to go with me, so we set another date to meet at the coffee shop.

We discussed more strategy that day over a cup of coffee, before we went to look for our man. We were disappointed to learn that he wasn't in. The secretary told us to sit down and we could talk to one of the other managers. My lawyer said, "I'm afraid we won't get any where if we have to talk to another man." The Lord showed us that He was with us. While we were waiting, the man we wanted to talk to came in. He invited us into his office and closed the door. The first thing he did was to call the receptionist and ask that no calls be passed on to him, because he would be in conference and didn't want to be disturbed. That made me nervous, but the lawyer took over. In no time at all the man pulled a form out of his desk and started filling it out. I didn't know it was that important signed statement that we needed. He said, "I'll make this out to say that it is valid provided that another payment is made before the last day of April." He signed his name to it, put his stamp on it, and handed it to the lawyer. Then we discussed the procedure for buying a van. He said the seller would have to come to the loan company office to sign the papers.

We went upstairs to make the payment but the business office was closed already. We still had time since the payment wasn't due till the end of April. I said, "I'll come in next week when I'm downtown and pay it." After that I would have ten days to find the van I wanted.

I went to the dealer to see how much a new van would cost. Horrors! The price had almost doubled since the first of January. I asked him if we could pay for part of it with the loan and pay the rest of it in payments to the dealer. He assured me that there would be no problem with that. I had doubts about whether the loan company would agree to that. When I went in to make the payment I talked to one of the managers about it. He was very inconsiderate and didn't even want to listen to my question. When he finally did, he didn't waste any words in telling me I couldn't do that. I talked to some other dealers and every time I ran into the same problem.

I realized that the only alternative was to look for a used van. I started searching the newspapers for a van like the one we wanted. There were very few listed. I started running all over town looking at everything that was for sale. That was another disappointment to me. Even used ones were too expensive. We now had less than 10 days. Prices were going up every day. Every day that passed meant that we would be buying less with the money we had. It was on a Thursday that I started looking at used vans. The first one that I looked at was a 1986 delivery van which meant that it didn't have seats in the back or windows. He wanted 55,000 Australes for it. I didn't give it much consideration. I went to see another one. It was what we wanted, but they were asking 68,000 Australes for it. That was far more than we could afford. I went to see a third one, but it had already sold before I got there. On Friday I started out early in the morning on the bus to look at more vans. The first one I saw was a beauty in a dealer's show room. It was all carpeted with lots of other luxuries. They were asking 70,000 Australes for it. I asked him about paying the balance in payments. He invited me to sit down at his desk and he pulled out his calculator and started figuring. In a little while he said, "If you are willing to mortgage your house I think we can do it." I asked him how much the payments would be. He worked with his calculator a little more and put the figures on paper. The payments would have been outrageous. I told him I wouldn't even consider that and walked out.

I went to another area of the city where there were many used car dealers. The only vans I found were of a brand in which I didn't have much confidence. I came home discouraged. I had other responsibilities on Saturday so I had to leave it until Monday. On Monday morning I took the car and went to check at some used car lots. I didn't have any leads at all and didn't have much hope of finding anything. As I expected, I didn't find anything. The next day the ten days would be up.

On Monday afternoon I had a lead to follow up, but it was a long ways away. Before I left, Margaret said, "Let's pray about it again." We prayed and I went and caught the bus. As I was riding on the bus my thoughts were troubled. I knew that it was almost certain that anything I found would be too expensive. Suddenly the thought came to me, "Why don't you reconsider the delivery van you saw last Saturday?" Then I thought, "No, it's almost certain that it's been sold by now." When I was there another man was looking at it. I debated about it and prayed about it for a few minutes longer. I decided to go. I got off the bus and crossed the street to go back the other way. I had to go several blocks back the way I had come to catch a bus to take me to where I saw the first van. It was the only one I had seen that was anywhere near a price we could afford. It was 5000 Australes more than the loan but maybe we could make up the difference.

When I arrived at the apartment house and rang the door bell, a voice came over the speaker asking, "Who is it?" I searched for words to identify myself. I said, "I came to see about the van you had for sale." I fully expected him to say, "It's sold." The only response was the buzz at the door to say I could come in. I went upstairs and knocked at their door and the man's wife answered. She asked me to wait a minute because her husband was on the phone. When he came I asked if the van had been sold, and he said it hadn't. I thought, "Since the Lord has answered that prayer there is certainly nothing wrong with asking if he would take less for it if we paid him in cash. He thought for a little bit and said we could have it for 52,000 Australes. I felt like shouting "Praise the Lord." I thought those two answers to prayer must be a clear indication that the Lord wanted us to have it. I said, "I'll take it." I asked for his phone number and told him I would talk to him that night after I had talked to my lawyer, to see when we could all meet at the loan company office.

When I called the lawyer he congratulated me for finding something at such a reasonable price. We agreed to meet at 5:00 the next afternoon at the loan company office. I called the seller and ask him to come. He asked if he should bring the van too. I'm glad I told him not to. Here's why:

The seller and his father were waiting at the coffee shop when I arrived. We drank coffee while we waited for the lawyer. When he arrived we crossed the street to complete the deal. We were in for the first of many surprises, when we sat down at the desk of the person who was in charge of making the transaction. She handed the lawyer a list of 8 requirements that she said must be met before the money could be released. The lawyer was somewhat indignant because they hadn't said anything about that before. He went over the list with her to make sure he understood all they were requiring. She said they didn't make all those demands on those who bought a vehicle from one of their approved dealers. It was obvious that they were doing everything possible to discourage us from buying from a private party. They weren't taking any chances. They wanted photo copies of all the papers on the van which had to be certified by a notary public whom they recommended.

The seller expressed his concern about accepting a check from the loan company. The lawyer tried to convince him that it was very doubtful that a big company like this would give him a bad check. He still insisted that it had to be a certified check, and they agreed to have a certified check ready for him the next day.

We left and went back to the coffee shop for more coffee and to discuss what must be done. The lawyer outlined carefully what the seller and I would have to do before we met again. Fortunately the seller was patient or maybe he just wanted the money badly enough to be willing to do all they asked of him. We had to get a statement from the government saying the taxes were paid, and that there were no leans against it.

The lawyer and I went to a public office which takes care of the transfer of titles of cars, and paid them to get that government document for us. They informed us that it would be Friday at the earliest and most likely Monday before we could have the document. The lawyer asked the girl to do all she could to have it ready by Friday.

The lawyer asked me to call him on Saturday evening to find out if everything was ready to make the deal on Monday. When I called he said everything was ready.

I think it was at 10:00 on Monday morning that we met at the coffee shop again. This meeting was just to make sure we had everything in order to make the deal. The woman looked over the papers to see if anything was lacking. In this type of operation the loan company doesn't keep the title. They fill out a paper that says the buyer can't sell it under any conditions, until he has met all the requirements of the loan company. That paper is called a "prenda." The lady said we would be signing it without it being filled out. My lawyer objected to that. She said, "But that's just standard procedure." The lawyer said, "We'll talk about that tomorrow."

Another requirement was that I had to have insurance on the van before we could make the deal. We knew there wouldn't be enough time on Monday to get all that done, so we planed to close the sale the next day. The loan company had an approved list of insurance companies. We picked out one and went to see about insurance. We called first to see if we would have to bring the van for them to see it. They said "no," but when we got there, they said the seller would have to bring it in for them to inspect it. He had to hurry home and get back there before closing time. I stayed to pay for the policy.

We all agreed to meet at the coffee shop the next morning at 10:00. At that meeting we discussed what we should do if they still insisted on my signing that prenda without it being filled out. The lawyer said I shouldn't sign it under such circumstances. He said they could put anything they wanted to in it once I had signed it. When we got to the office the lady brought it in blank and asked me to sign it. I refused. She said again, "But it's standard procedure." I said, "I'd be a fool not to take the lawyer's advice. The lawyer asked why it had to be signed in blank. She said it was to save time. The lawyer said, "Well we aren't going to sign it in blank. We'll take time to wait for you to fill it out." She said, "Well if you want to wait an hour we can get it filled out." The lawyer said, "That's fine." Before going in that morning the lawyer said, "If they refuse to fill out that prenda we can go to the police and report it, because it's illegal to sign a paper in blank.

We went back an hour later. This is when the high point of the drama began. The lady asked the lawyer if he would like to read the prenda. He said, "Of course I would." I was in hopes he would find everything in order, that we could sign the papers, and go home with the van that day. I could see that he was reading and rereading some lines. I assumed something must be wrong. The lady at the desk was occupied by a phone call. When she finished, he said, "Excuse me but this isn't right. The way this is filled out my client would be obligated to pay 36,000 Australes plus 19 payments of

1,892 Australes. Actually all he should be obligated to pay are the payments." In Spanish the words "and/or" are written "y/o". The paper should have been written to say I could fulfill my obligation either by paying 36,000 Australes or 19 payments of 1982 Australes. They just had the "y" and had left out the "o". The woman insisted that that was the way it had to be. The lawyer said, "Wait a minute," and went out to talk to the man who had given us the signed statement, to say we could have the money. He didn't get any satisfaction from him and he came back in to say, "Let's go fellows."

I knew where we were going, but he didn't tell the lady at the desk. As we went up the stairs the man the lawyer had talked to was standing there and he said to me, "You are making an awful mistake." I replied, "I don't think so." The lawyer had told him what we were going to do and that man knew where we were going.

When we got outside he said, "Let's go find the nearest police station and denounce them." We walked about a block and found a policeman, and he directed us to the police station. When we got there they said we would have to go to a different station. We went to the street again following the lawyer. He was in a hurry. I was behind him and the seller and his father were behind me.

We had gone about two blocks and I could see that he and his father were lingering behind. The seller called to the lawyer and said, "Look, I'm ready to quit. If this has to go through the hands of the police it will go to the courts, and it will take months to get a settlement." It was then that we learned that the seller had already made a down payment on a car he wanted to buy. He was counting on getting the money from us that day to finish paying for the car. If he didn't, he was in danger of losing the money he had put down on it. The lawyer debated a little bit and said, "Let's go and talk to the loan company's lawyer. We stopped the first taxi that came by and the lawyer gave him directions to the office of the loan company's lawyer.

We had only gone a few blocks when the seller got nervous and began sticking his hands in all his pockets. I thought maybe he had an itch. He said, "Oh no, what did I do with the keys to the van?" He looked in his brief case and didn't find them. Then he said, "Maybe I left them on the desk of that lady at the loan company office." The lawyer told the taxi driver to turn around and take us back to the loan company office. When we got there he jumped out and went in to get them. When he didn't come back right away the lawyer suspected something was wrong. After awhile the seller returned with the keys. All he said was that "they were starting to soften up a little bit."

When we went back down stairs the woman was there who had written the prenda. She was much more humble. She admitted she had made a mistake. I guess we will never know if it was a mistake or not. Anyway she agreed to do it again, and do it right. It was near closing time, so we decided we would have to come back the next day.

We went back to the coffee shop and the seller tried to call the dealer where he was buying the car to plead for mercy for another day. He didn't get any answer. The lawyer had other commitments, so he said we would have to wait till 4:00 the next afternoon to meet. Margaret had gone with us on Monday and had signed her name on the prenda. They said she would have to come back again since they had to tear up the first prenda and make a new one.

When we all got together again the next day we asked ourselves what tricks they would try to pull on us this time. The lawyer read the prenda over carefully. He said, "It's filled out right this time except that some blank spaces will have to be crossed out, so that nothing more can be added later. They agreed to do that. The original prenda was torn up in front of us. They called the seller into the office and gave him his money. After I paid to get the van out of the parking lot I only had 10 Australes left.

We were relieved to get into our van. When I looked at the needle on the dash board, it showed that the gas tank was empty. I said to Margaret, "How are we going to get home with this without any gas?" We pulled into the first gas station we came to and put in 10 Australes worth of gas. It still showed empty. We prayed that we would arrive home with the little gas we had in the tank. If not, we wouldn't even have enough money to go on the bus or make a telephone call. The Lord helped us. He never fails! We arrived at the church just as the people were gathering for the Wednesday evening service. We had much thanks to give to our dear Lord that evening.

Later we put seats and windows in the van so we could use it for the church. The rate of exchange was in our favor. The payment I made on the van in December was $371. When I made the last payment a year and a half later it was only about $5.00. That's because the Argentine money had lost that much in value. We later converted the van to natural gas which made it more economical. To God be the glory! "And let us not be weary in well doing; for in due season we shall reap, if we faint not." Gataltians 6:9

A Mission Of Mercy

We can't serve God without serving people. Sometimes that involves doing things we'd rather not do. I had one of those experiences on New Years day, 1992. It involved Andrew, a man who made a profession of faith about 10 days previously while in the hospital awaiting a gall bladder operation. Andrew's wife, Hilda, was a faithful Christian who had been attending our church for several years. He made a profession of faith a number of years ago, but we never saw anything to indicate it was genuine. He beat his wife and more than once threatened to kill her. More than once she came to church in tears, and said that Andrew had kicked her out of the house and told her not to come back again. Each time I prayed with her and consoled her, and told her to return home, acting like nothing had ever happened. When ever I tried to talk to Andrew he would agree with everything I told him, but there was no indication of repentance.

Andrew had an operation and was discharged from the hospital. I took him home on Saturday and he seemed to be on his way to recovery. The following Monday I took him back to the hospital for a check up. After waiting for over an hour, they finally told him to go back home, because they weren't going to be able to see him that morning. By Tuesday afternoon he was suffering a lot so we took him back to the hospital. That time they dressed his incision and sent him back home. They told him he should get a nurse to come the next day and dress his incision. While we were at the hospital it began to rain hard. We left the hospital through flooded streets and a driving rain. I took him to our house first because I was afraid I couldn't get to his house. They lived about a half mile off the pavement. Juan Carlos, the pastor of our first church, was working at our house and I thought it would be best to take him along. We waited for a while for the rain to stop but, when it appeared that it wasn't going to, we went ahead with him.

The next afternoon, New Years day, we were spending a quiet afternoon at home. My wife woke me up from a nap to tell me that Hilda and her daughter had come to ask me to take Andrew back to the hospital. Juan Carlos had wrecked our van the night before, so we didn't have any transportation. They went to find a nurse who attends our church, but she wasn't home. They were considering going to the hospital to see if they could get an ambulance to come out and get him. I was certain that they wouldn't succeed in finding an ambulance, since it was New Years day. Also, because it had been raining all day, it would be impossible to get to their house with an ambulance.

I felt the Lord telling me that I should go and dress his incision. I'm not a doctor, not even a nurse. In Bible College I had a one semester course in missionary medicine. There didn't seem to be any solution. Finally I said, "If you want, I'll go and do it." Hilda, was in agreement with that. I took a bottle with a few Tylenol tablets in it out of the medicine cabinet, put on my boots, grabbed an umbrella and started out with them. I walked the four blocks to the highway and took a bus to the end of the bus line. From there, it's normally about 6 blocks they have to walk to their house, but because of the flooding, I had to walk about a mile to get there. The farther I went the deeper the water got. Fortunately my boots were high enough to get me through. The house was completely surrounded by water; 6-8 inches deep in places.

I clasped Andrew's hand and prayed with him. I told him what I was going to do and he was in agreement. I ask Hilda for a pan of water and soap to wash my hands. I warned Andrew that it was going to hurt when I removed the bandage. Hilda held one of his arms and I held the other one. With my free hand I ripped off the bandage. I washed the incision with soap and water the best I knew how. We also did something that is quite unconventional, but common procedure in Argentina. We put sugar on the incision, covered it with gauze, and taped it down. They say the sugar makes it heal faster. I gave Andrew two Tylenol tablets to relieve the pain. That was the only time I had to dress Andrew's incision. The next time a nurse did it. She said it looked as though I did a good job dressing his incision.

Argentine Funerals

People die in much the same way all over the world, but in various parts of the world they have many and diverse means of expressing their grief and paying their last respects to their departed loved ones. More than once I have seen grown men express their grief by throwing themselves on the ground, kicking and screaming, like a child in a temper tantrum. Due to mitigating circumstances, two funerals I had a part in were not typical argentine funerals.

The first funeral was for our neighbor's wife who lived across the street. She was the mother of seven children. The children attended our church quite regularly and she came occasionally. She died suddenly due to, what some thought was, a local doctor's mistake. Someone found her lying in the street about two blocks from her house. They ran to the doctor's house close by. He gave her a shot for what he thought was low blood pressure and had someone take her to the hospital. We heard what had happened about 6:00 in the evening. Margaret went over and prayed with the children. We didn't know any more about it until 4:00 the next morning, when someone rang our door bell and informed us that she had died. We dressed quickly and went over there. Margaret had the responsibility of telling the oldest girl the sad news that her mother had died. I left with her husband to go to inform some of the relatives of the death. There were very few telephones back then. We returned back about 7:00 in the morning. Then her husband went to make funeral arrangements. I offered to let them have the funeral in the back room of our house, which also served as the meeting place for our church.

An Argentine funeral is not a formal service like we have in the States. It is more like what is called a wake. The body is displayed in the open casket and people come to visit. It is very rare that a body is embalmed. The law says burial must take place within 24 hours after the death. It occasionally goes longer than that.

We prepared the church room and waited for them to bring the body. As I recall, they arrived around noon with it. I stood beside her casket with the broken hearted husband and father, and prayed that God would comfort him and give him wisdom to raise his children without his wife's help. Neighbors, relatives and friends began to arrive.

Our house was filled with people, many of whom we had never met. I read Scripture and prayed. Our only bath room was normally busy with our family of 6 children, but now we sometimes had to stand in line to use it.

The 24 hours wouldn't be up until some time in the night. Of course they don't bury people at night. We expected the funeral people would come and take the body to the cemetery the first thing the next morning. The custom is for some of the close relatives to sit up with the body all night. We told them to go to the kitchen to heat water for coffee in the night if they wanted to.

Our family went to bed. There was a window between our bedroom and the church room. The shutters were closed to give us privacy but we could still hear them talking. We slept anyhow since we had been up since 4:00 the previous morning.

I awoke early the next morning to the sound of rain. I heard another sound that bothered me. It was the sound of someone pushing water with a rubber squeegee on a broom handle. They are used to scrub the floors in the Argentine homes so they are just as common as the broom.

When it rained hard we often had a problem with flooding at our house. In many sections of the city there are no storm sewers. They count on the streets to carry the water away. All the sewage water from the houses, except from the bathroom stools, is piped out to the street to drain away. Our house was almost on the level of the street. When it rained hard the street filled up with water and backed up into our house. I often had to plug up the drain pipe with plastic bags.

When I heard someone pushing water that morning I knew what it meant. I got up, dressed, and went out to see what I could do to help. Water was already about an inch deep under the casket. The people didn't have a dry inch of floor to stand on. Some were barefooted. I dashed out to the storage room and brought in a little pump to see if I could pump the water out. Due to the hard rain the water was coming in faster than I could pump it out.

The back room of our house was always the first to flood. The rest of the house was still dry. We decided to move the casket and everything to the front room of our house, which also served as our living room. One of the family's relatives was sleeping on the sofa in there. He or she, I'm not sure which it was, had to be awakened first. As soon as the room was unoccupied we started moving. All the men helped carry the casket. We had to take it through our kitchen and lift it up over the kitchen table. We sat it on the floor and went back to get the metal stand to set it on. Then we brought in the wreaths of flowers and everything else that goes with a funeral.

It was all to no avail. The rain didn't stop. It was one of the worst floods we ever had. The street and sidewalk were under water. The only way to get into our house was by wading through water 6 inches deep. By 10:00 in the morning there wasn't a dry inch of floor in the whole house. Water was running in the back door and going out the front door. It was finally decided that we had better take the body across the street to the family's house. Their house was on a little higher elevation and it wasn't flooded. Rather than carry everything across the flooded street, I backed our Jeep wagon up into the driveway. Our drive way was higher and wasn't under water. We loaded the casket in the wagon and took it across the street. I made another trip to get the flowers and other paraphernalia. The men pulled up their pants legs and waded across. Everyone was wet and cold.

It stopped raining shortly after that, but the funeral cars didn't arrive until about 2:00 in the afternoon. By that time the water in the street had gone down some. I took some of the neighbors to the cemetery in our jeep wagon. Others went in pickup trucks. It's not unusual to see 15-20 people standing in the back of a pickup going to the cemetery.

The burial at the cemetery was the standard procedure. It always seems to me that the funeral people are in a hurry to get the body unloaded so they can go and haul in another one. They call on whatever men are close by to carry the body to the burial site. The open grave has two planks laid across it to rest the casket on. Normally there are no rites or formalities at the cemetery. While all the people are standing around, the cemetery people put ropes under the casket and lower it into the grave. The top of the casket is only about 18 inches below the ground. As soon as the ropes are pulled out the people start picking up clods of dirt that they throw onto the casket. It is a solemn sound to hear those clods of dirt go thud, thud on the top of the wooden box. Then the cemetery men approach with their shovels and quickly cover the casket. The wreaths of flowers are thrown on the grave and it's all over. One by one the people, some weeping or sobbing, make their way back to their cars.

There was another funeral for a man who's name was Roger. I expect he must have been around 30 years old when he died. His wife, Rose, and the children had been attending our church. Roger attended occasionally.

One rainy morning someone rang the door bell and I went to answer the door. It was a brother in law of Rose. When he told me that Roger had died I had to ask him again what he had said, because I couldn't believe I heard him right. He said Roger had a heart attack and died suddenly. Some said the heart attack was brought on because of a violent argument he had with his wife.

Margaret and I put on our boots and took our umbrellas and walked the 8 blocks to Rose's house. She had gone to make funeral arrangements and we didn't stay long. When we arrived home we called Juan Carlos on our C.B. radio. That afternoon he and his wife came over, and we drove over to Rose's house. We had to leave the car about 4 blocks away, because of the muddy streets, and walk the rest of the way. The body was on display in the living room. Rose was in bed and didn't come out all the time we were there. We assured them that we would come back that evening with some others from the church. Some of the women from the church went with us that evening. It was still raining. We had to leave the car and walk in. While we were there it rained even harder. I remember standing at the front door and watching the frogs hop around in the grass. At the same time I remember thanking God that we were privileged to be in Argentina where people needed us. Rose was still in bed. As I recall, Margaret and some of the other women went in and talked to her. Most likely I read some Scripture and prayed with the people who were gathered there.

When it became apparent that the rain wasn't going to let up, we trudged back to our car under what little protection our umbrellas offered us. It was a relief to get into the car and out of the rain. We had only gone a few blocks down the street before we met a man walking up the street. He stopped us to tell us that the street was flooded and we wouldn't be able to get through, but we didn't take him seriously. About an hour and a half before that there hadn't been enough water in the street to hinder us from going through. About two blocks farther on, we started driving through water. We thought if we go slowly there is no reason why we can't get through. It kept getting deeper. About a half a block before we got to the highway one of the women said, "It's coming in through the doors." A few seconds later one said; "Oh, it's clear up to the seats." About that time the car stalled because the exhaust pipe was under water. We got out in water up to our waists and pushed the car up onto the highway. What a relief it was when the motor started. The seats were saturated with water but we got in and went on anyway. We found other streets flooded and had to leave the people to walk the last few blocks to their houses. Margaret and I came on home and drove the car into the garage. The next morning water was still dripping out of the car and running out under the garage door. We couldn't use the car until we got the seats dried out. We had to take them all out and leave them in the sun for several days to dry.

The next morning Margaret and I walked over to Rose's house. Juan Carlos and others went on the bus. The rain had stopped but there was still mud everywhere. Rose was still in bed. We persuaded her to get up and come out. For several hours that day we had to be at her side constantly. Every now and then she fainted. We had to bend her forward, slap her face, or tip her chair back. One lady had some strong perfume that she would hold under her nose when she started to faint. The next door neighbor was a fireman and he had some knowledge of what to do. We weren't having much success so we finally sent Juan Carlos to get a doctor. After what seemed like hours, he returned with a doctor that we knew. He gave her some medicine, but we couldn't tell that it helped much.

It was well past the 24 hours and the funeral people still hadn't arrived to take the body to the cemetery. We debated about what to do with Rose when they did come. How would we get her to the cemetery? Would it be best to leave someone at the house with her? If she couldn't walk the 4 blocks out to the paved street we would have to carry her.

Rose and Roger's children were at a neighbor's house and hadn't even seen their father in the casket. In the afternoon we finally convinced Rose that they should be brought to see their father before the body was taken away. When they brought the children to the back door, I picked up the boy and carried him in to see his father. I did the best I could to explain to him that he wasn't going to see his daddy again.

When the funeral people finally arrived we lifted Rose onto her feet to see if she could walk. We decided we had better take a chair so we could set her down in case she should lose consciousness on the way. It was a solemn procession that made its way up the muddy street. The fireman and I accompanied Rose, one on each side to give her support. Other men carried the casket. Some carried wreaths of flowers and other articles of funeral equipment. One carried the chair.

Rose made it to the paved street and we seated her in the funeral car. Margaret and I and others had to catch a bus to go to the cemetery. We had our doubts that we would get there in time, but we did.

Funerals give us a chance to minister to the living, but it's often difficult to comfort the bereaved if their departed loved one has never made a profession of salvation. As the Apostle Paul said in II Corintians 13:8, "We can do nothing against the truth, but for the truth."

Funerals in Argentina are never easy. We never know what to expect. Thankfully, not all of them have been as hectic as the two I have told you about.

The Continuing Impact of a Missionary's Life and Labor

The Continuing Impact of
a missionary's life and labor

As a young man I heard some one say "Every time you spend time with some one you change that person in some measure. I have often thought of the truth of that statement. I'm sure I would need to recognize that there is also a vice versa to the statement. In other words, if I spend time with someone, that person will change my life in some measure also. The more time we spend with someone, the more opportunity we have to change his or her life.

As missionaries, our goal should be that of changing lives. We are not interested in what we can get from people. To the contrary, our goal is to give something to people. People need what we have and we need to convince them that they need it. The good part is that what we have to give to others makes them richer, but it doesn't make us any poorer.

The change we want to make in the life of those around us is brought about by introducing them to Jesus Christ. Once they accept him as their Savior and surrender their lives to him he begins working in their lives. II Corinthians 5:17 says "Therefore if any man be in Christ, he is a new creature: old things are passed away; behold, all things are become new." Ephesians 2:10 says "For we are his workmanship, created in Christ Jesus unto good works, which God hath before ordained that we should walk in them."

Being surrendered to God is a continuing struggle for all of us. For that reason, we need to spend time with people. First we have to win their confidence. If not, they won't even listen to us. We may need to spend time just being their friend. They have to see that we have something to offer them. The natural man has his eyes on material things. If I make friends with a man, many times his first thoughts are in what I have to offer him from an economic standpoint. That's where our friendship often breaks down because when a man doesn't find any material advantage to being my friend he isn't interested in developing the friendship. We may need to make friends with a great number of people to find some who will stay with us long enough to realize that the best we have to offer them is spiritual and not material.

I was saved because I met some young people at the University of Nebraska who had joy in life and a reason for living that I didn't have. They were more or less on the same economic level that I was. Therefore I couldn't expect to gain much economically from them. I realized that spiritual values were important to them. For me, spiritual things had no importance. I saw no need of them. By observing the life of these friends I finally realized that their relationship with God was what made them different. Because of that, the day finally came when I too accepted Jesus Christ as my Savior and surrendered my life to him.

I have four sisters and no brothers. I could have taken over my parent's ranch in the Sand Hills of Nebraska. If I had done so, I would no doubt have been successful in accumulating wealth, but I would have missed the opportunity of making an impact on a great number of people in this world. When I was a boy our work was centered around the farm. We nearly always went into town one day a week to sell the cream and eggs and do our shopping. There were times in the busy summer months when six days would go by when we wouldn't see anyone outside of our family. A farmer spends long hours on a tractor in his fields. His greatest impact is on his wife and children. It's not that that isn't important.

Even before becoming a Christian I made an important decision. I was studying agriculture at the University of Nebraska. I decided that I wanted to spend my life working with people and not with plants and animals. That's what kept me from staying on the farm.

Over the years we have made the acquaintance of hundreds of people, both in Argentina and in the States. They have contributed something to us, but I would like to think we have also contributed something to them. It's a mutual contribution. It may be that people in the States have contributed more to us than we have to them. The Argentine people have taught us much, but I would like to think that we have contributed more to them than they have to us.

It's our desire that what we contribute to others will go on making an impact on their lives. We want our fruit to remain as Jesus said in John 15:16. "Ye have not chosen me, but I have chosen you, and ordained you, that ye should go and bring forth fruit, and that your fruit should remain: that whatsoever ye shall ask of the Father in my name, he may give it you." For that reason, we plant churches and train leaders who will carry on where we leave off. Jesus sends us forth to make disciples. The word "teach" in the great commission in Matthew 28:18-20, really means "make disciples." The plan of God is that his work be perpetual. II Timothy 2:2 says "And the things that thou hast heard of me among many witnesses, the same commit thou to faithful men, who shall be able to teach others also."

In theory, a missionary's work should go on expanding. He should work to that end. By studying history, however, we see that works that began well don't always end well. Because of sin and the negligence of God's people, churches, schools and outreach ministries deteriorate over a period of time. New works must be begun to replace those that have departed from the course. We should not be discouraged if that happens.

Recently we received communication from a young lady who was a part of one of our churches in Argentina many years ago. Her name is Andrea. She is now a receptionist at a doctor's office. We had lost contact with her for many years. We had to guess at who she was. Further contact with her confirmed that our guess was right. She and her family were a part of our church. We made many sacrifices on their behalf. We had reason to think that our sacrifices were in vain. What we did for her was not forgotten.

We can think of others we ministered to as children who are now adults, but they are still going on for God. Some are people I baptized. With some, I performed their weddings. It's a consolation to know that all was not lost. We try not to dwell on those who have fallen away. I'm wondering if one of the thrills of heaven may be to meet people whose lives we have touched. They may come up to us with a big smile on their face, give us a hug, and say, "I wouldn't be here if it weren't for what you did." That's part of the treasure we are laying up in heaven. "Lay not up for yourselves treasures upon earth, where moth and rust doth corrupt, and where thieves break through and steal: But lay up for yourselves treasures in heaven, where neither moth nor rust doth corrupt, and where thieves do not break through nor steal: For where your treasure is, there will your heart be also" (Matthew 6:19-21).

God is no respecter of persons. I don't for a moment think that we missionaries will get greater rewards in heaven than others. In God's vineyard there is a place for all his children to labor. That farmer I mentioned earlier who spends his days on his tractor in his fields can have part in it too. It may be that he and his wife have imparted a love for God to their children, and some day one or more of them will surrender their lives to work in God's vineyard. It may be also that he has given a part of the fruits of his labor to make it possible for missionaries to go forth. Many are the housewives who spend time praying for missionaries. There are many avenues of service for those who love God and want to serve him. We are all part of God's team.

A Tribute To
Our Children

A Tribute to Our Children

It's very possible that the contribution we have made to the Lord's work will be extremely small in comparison to that which our children have made and will yet make. We are greatly indebted to them. Some missionaries are criticized by people in the States for having too many children. Their thinking is that it costs too much to send a big family to the mission field. It's true that it does cost more, but children can be a tremendous asset to missionaries. Our six children worked right along side of us in the work on the mission field. When it came time for church they went out to invite and bring in the neighbor children. They often went out about a half hour early to remind them because many of them didn't know what time it was. Our children carried all the chairs in the house into the church room and set everything up for the service. When it was over they put them all back. They distributed the hymn books and put them away afterward. Margaret made a weekly list of jobs to do around the house.

When our children were old enough, they started leading singing and teaching Sunday school classes. Most of our boys learned to preach in their teens. For a time we had a boy's club. We met once a week, many times under a tree in the back yard. We did a lot of fun things together.

Debra

Debra was our firstborn. She was 12 years old when we arrived in Argentina. I can hardly remember when she wasn't a Sunday school teacher. She loves to work with children. After high school she went to the States to go to college. After graduating from Bible College she taught in a Christian day school for a year and a half. Then a missionary family in Argentina invited her to return to Argentina and teach their children. She went back as a missionary teacher and taught for several years. She lived with us all the years when we were in Argentina. She was also our piano player. We thank the Lord for the tremendous asset she was been to our work. She is still in Argentina serving as a single missionary.

Kevin

One Father's Day Kevin became part of our family. He has a keen mind and is a good student. Apart from what we could teach him, he learned to be an electronic engineer. When he was still in high school he worked at a little airport near our house fixing the navigation radios in small planes. When he finished high school, he too came to the States to work. A year later he decided to go to Bible College. He never felt inclined to work full time in the Lord's work. His interests were in electronics. After graduating from Bible College he married a girl he met there. He worked at several jobs until he decided to move to Phoenix, Arizona to work and help in a Spanish ministry in a church. They had two sons before his first wife died of cancer. About four years later he married a girl he knew in Argentina. Her name is Daiana. He took her back to the States where she quickly learned to speak English and live in a different culture. For a time Kevin had a job fixing and selling scales. Then he worked at an airport fixing flight instruments on airplanes. Now he is the designer and manufacturer of equipment that he sells to airports to be used in testing navigation instruments in airplanes. They now have seven children including the two he had from his first wife. They are active in a good Baptist church.

Brian

Right from the start, Brian was our preacher boy. While still in high school he and I would go with the young people in our church to preach on the street in down town Laferrere. One time Brian was preaching on hell in a plaza across the street from the municipality. To illustrate the point, he took along a five gallon paint pail filled with wood scraps that he set on fire. While he was preaching a policeman came over from the municipality. We expected that he was going to chase us out of there. Instead, he suggested that we set the pail of burning wood on some bricks so it wouldn't damage the sidewalk. After going to Bible College Brian married Liesl, his college sweet heart, and they went out to raise support to go to Argentina as a missionaries. He started a church in the capital city of the province of Buenos Aires. He is working as co-pastor with another missionary in the northern part of Argentina where they have a seminary to train preacher boys. They have five children.

Darrell

Darrell was a super active child and the greatest challenge for his parents. He was always looking for adventure. He came back to the States to work for his uncle. Later he went to Bible College for one semester. Then he joined the U. S. Army. While in basic training he met Alma and they were married before he was sent on his first overseas assignment. They have one daughter. Fortunately he never had to go to war but he served a number of years in overseas military bases. We felt honored to have a son serving in the defense of our country. He finally decided he had enough of the Army. He got out and joined the Border Patrol in Arizona. He stayed in the reserves and was called back in and sent to Kuwait. After that tour of duty he returned to the Border Patrol and was eventually transferred to Duluth, Minnesota where he is presently. He is active in a church there.

Calvin

Calvin was almost three years old when we arrived in Argentina. He spent his childhood and teen years there except when we came back to the States a few times for a furlough. After he finished high school he came back to the States to go to Bible College. When he graduated he went to Denver, Colorado to help a church begin a Spanish ministry. Later he felt led of the Lord to go to Puerto Rico to help a pastor-missionary.

There he taught in a Bible College and pastored a small church. He felt inadequate for two reasons. First he felt he needed to further his education to be better able to teach in the Bible College. Another need he felt was that of a wife to be a better pastor. He returned to the States and enrolled in another Bible College to get further training. While there he met Jennifer. After they were married they went out to raise support to return to Puerto Rico as missionaries. They are still serving there where both are active in a teaching ministry as well as helping in church planting. They now have four children. Calvin has also felt a burden to go to Cuba as a missionary. He has gone there several times, but is unable to live there

Priscila

Priscila was born in Argentina. Her only experience with American life was when we brought her back to the States on furloughs. She, as well as her brothers, attended Christian day schools during those times. She has a love for little children. She has been a tremendous help to us as a teacher in the nursery department. Children make up to her almost immediately. She took some courses in a Bible college in Argentina. For a time she taught English. She was a tremendous help to us in the early days of getting Hope Baptist Church started. It was during that time that she met Javier whom she married. Javier was also a tremendous help to us in the early days of Hope Baptist church. They now have one daughter.

Statement of Purpose

What we did in the years we spent in Argentina is really the story of what God did in and through us. In and of ourselves, we weren't capable of doing anything. We would have to say with the Apostol Paul, "For I know that in me (that is in my flesh,) dwelleth no good thing: for to will is present with me; but how to perform that which is good I find not." (Romans 7:18) What we did, could have been done better. We could have done much more than we did. We don't save souls, God does with our help. Were it not for the grace and goodness of God we wouldn't have done anything for God. All he needs is a willing soul. What he did in and through us, he could do for you if you would surrender your life to him.

This book was written with a double purpose. First, and foremost, it is to glorify God. "Thou art worthy, O Lord, to receive glory and honor and power: for thou hast created all things, and for thy pleasure they are and were created." Revelation 4:11 Even the best of God's children are not capable of offering him the glory he deserves.

The second purpose for the book is that you, my reader, might come to see your need of the great salvation. In Hebrews 2:3 the Bible says "How shall we escape, if we neglect so great salvation; which at the first began to be spoken by the Lord, and was confirmed unto us by them that heard him." The judgment of God rests upon us because we are sinners. Romans 3:23 says "For all have sinned, and come short of the glory of god." That includes you too, my friend. By Jesus sacrificial death on the cross we can be forgiven of our sins and be received into the family of God. Salvation is the gift of God. It's not by means of anything we can do. Ephesians 2:8-9 says, "For by grace are ye saved through faith; and that not of yourselves: it is the gift of God: not of works, lest any man should boast." All we need to do to have it is to repent of our sins, trust in Christ, and ask God to save us. Acts 3:19 says, "Repent ye therefore, and be converted, that your sins may be blotted out, when the times of refreshing shall come from the presence of the Lord."

If you have been saved or blessed in some way by this book we would be thrilled to know about it. If we can be of some help in your spiritual life please feel free to let us know of your need. On the back cover of the book you will find a way to communicate with us.

Russell's Believe It Or Not

Russell's Believe It Or Not

When I was a boy I enjoyed reading "Ripley's Believe it or Not which always appeared on the comic page of the newspaper. Robert Ripley traveled all over the world and reported on unusual phenomenon. He expected people to believe his reports. If you choose not to believe my stories in this supplement I won't be offended.

This supplement is meant to be a reward for having read my book. It's like desert you get after cleaning up your plate. Now if you haven't read my book yet, please, please, go back to page one and read the book like it was meant to be read.

Thanks

The Hybrid Lima Beans

One year my mother ordered some hybrid lima beans from the seed catalogue. The catalogue said they were the most amazing beans that had ever been bred. My dad planted them down by a corn field. We had a dry summer and the beans didn't do well. The grass hoppers ate some of them. When it came time to harvest them we only got a tin can full.

My mother put them up on a shelf and forgot about them. One cold winter day she saw them on the shelf when she was looking for something else. She said to herself. "I should cook those for our dinner tomorrow." As is the custom with beans, she put them in a pan to soak over night before being cooked the next day. She thought, "There are hardly enough to make a meal for our family." She decided to bake some corn bread to eat with them.

The next morning, when she got up, she found a disaster in the kitchen. Those beans had swollen up and pushed themselves right out of the pan. There were beans all over the floor. Some were on the counter. Only one was left in the pan.

She rounded up enough pans to be able to cook one bean for each one of us in the family. She gathered up the rest of them in a bushel basket and fed them to the pigs. When she cooked the beans they swelled up even more. Each bean was a plate full in itself. She gave up making corn bread. We ate bean for dinner.

My mother wanted to order more of those lima beans to plant in her garden the next year. When the seed catalogue came out they weren't listed. She wrote to the seed company and asked why they had quit selling them. They wrote back and said the grass hoppers had eaten all their breeding stock.

The Giant Corn Stalk

When I was a boy my parents expected me to help with the chores around the farm. They always milked six to eight cows. They ran the milk through a separator to separate the cream from the skim milk. The cream was kept in a cream can in the cellar because it was a little cooler there. The skim milk was fed to the calves and the pigs. Once a week we took the cream into town to sell it.

One Saturday morning, in the month of May, my dad sent me to feed a pail of milk to the pigs. The night before he had put some corn in the pail with the milk to let it soak. He said it made the pigs grow faster. Normally I had to carry a big stick in one hand to fight the pigs off so I could dump the milk in their trough. This particular morning they were still sleeping. They heard me dump the milk in the trough and came running. Before they got to the trough I noticed that one kernel of corn was swelled up about twice as big as the rest of the kernels. I reached down and grabbed it before the pigs got there. I put it in my pocket and went on my way.

After breakfast that morning I went to the field with my dad. He was planting corn. He planted corn with what was called a lister. The machine left furrows and ridges with the corn planted at the bottom of the furrow. He pulled it with a team of horses. I followed along behind with a tin can in my hand to pick up the grub worms that appeared from time to time as he opened the furrow. I took them home for the chickens. They went wild over them.

About noon my dad said, "Well, I expect we better go home for dinner." Just then I noticed that my right front pocket was all swollen up. It was then that I remembered that I had put that kernel of corn in my pocket when I fed the pigs. I couldn't get my hand in my pocket to take it out. I showed it to my dad. He couldn't get it out either. He said, "Well son, I guess we will have to take your pants down and rip the pocket open to get it out of there." I took my pants down and he reached in his pocket and brought out his pocket knife. He cut the pocket from top to bottom to get that kernel of corn out. It was about the size of a grown man's hand. We stood and looked at it in amazement. I said, "Let's plant it and see if it will grow." With my hand I dug a hole at the end of the row and threw it in and covered it up. On the way home I said to my dad, "It's a good thing one of the pigs didn't swallow that kernel whole. It would have stopped up his bowels." At the dinner table we told my mother and sisters about it. My dad said, "There is no chance that it will grow after it's been soaked in milk over night."

After dinner my dad got the horses out of the barn and we went back to the field. When we got back to where we left off we were amazed at what we found. That kernel of corn had already sprouted and was already standing about an inch out of the ground. I stuck a stick in the ground to mark the spot and we went on planting corn. That evening, on the way back to the house, we noticed that that corn stalk was already about six inches tall. You wouldn't believe how fast that corn stalk grew. Every day it shot up a few feet higher.

About a month later Billy, a neighbor friend of mine, came over to our house on Barney, his horse, to go rabbit hunting with me. Before he got to our house he scarred up a rabbit. He tied his horse to what he thought was a tree. He grabbed his gun, crawled under the fence, and went out into the pasture to see if he could find that rabbit. He didn't find the rabbit so he went back to get his horse and come on over to our house. When he got back to where he left Barney, he wasn't there. He walked on over to our house. When I saw him he had a sad look on his face. I said, "What's wrong, Billy?" He said, "It's Barney. I tied him to a tree along side of the road and when I came back to get him he wasn't there." I said, "I think I know where he might be. Let me get my gun and some ammunition and we'll go look for him." We walked back up the road to where the giant corn stalk was. Sure enough, there was old Barney hanging up in the corn stalk, kicking for all he was worth. Billy said, "How are we going to get him down out of there?" I said, "Hand me your gun and I'll see if I can shoot the rope and cut it." Every time I shot, it scarred Barney half to death. He thought we were shooting at him. It took several shots before I weakened the rope enough that it broke and let Barney fall down. When he fell it knocked the wind out of him and he lay there puffing and pawing for a few minutes before he got up. He didn't appear to have any broken bones.

During the summer the corn stalk was a tourist attraction. On Saturdays and Sundays we stood at the gate and charged admission. We let cars in for 50 cents and charged people 10 cents if they walked in. We opened a gate in the pasture to make a place for parking. Some times there were fifty or sixty cars parked in there on a Sunday afternoon. Some people came and had a picnic under the shade of the corn stalk. It was a good source of income.

In the fall the stalk was so tall that we couldn't see the top of it on a cloudy day. It started setting ears about every ten feet. They were giant ears; about the size of a truck bed. We wondered how we would harvest the crop. Around the first of October we had a killing frost and everything turned brown, including the corn stalk.

Back in those days we still picked corn by hand. We used a team and wagon. The horses pulled the wagon slowly through the field, as the farmer picked two rows at a time and threw the ears into the wagon. The wagons were equipped with what was called a bang board. It consisted of several boards the length of the wagon attached to one side of it so the ears could be thrown against it, and they would fall into the wagon. When I returned from school in the afternoon I helped my dad for about an hour finish up the afternoon wagon load. I also helped on Saturdays. We could pick two loads a day.

When the neighbors finished with their corn harvest that fall a number of them came to our place one Saturday to cut down the giant corn stalk. They all brought their axe. They started around noon chopping at it. They spent all afternoon working on it. In the evening I had to go to the house to do the chores. While I was milking a cow I heard them shout "Timber." About a half hour later that corn stalk hit the ground like a crash of thunder. Dust rose high in the sky. Before it got dark the neighbors took their axes and cut off a few of the ears. They were about 30 feet long.

What we thought was a happy ending turned out to be a sad story. The next morning neighbors from miles away arrived to notify my dad that they were going to take him to court. One said, "That corn stalk fell on my barn and smashed it." Another said "It fell on my herd of cows and killed four of them." Another said "It fell across my road and I have to go miles around to get into town." The only consolation my dad could give them was to say, "You can have all the ears of corn that fell on your land." He didn't have money to pay for the damage that was done. Some one called it a "disaster area." That gave him an idea. He said, "I'll write to the president and tell him what happened to see if he can give us some relief." About a week after he mailed the letter the president flew out in his airplane and looked over the area. Sure enough, he called it a disaster area and the government paid the damages.

The Stinken Fish Bait

The summer after I graduated from high school I agreed to work for a neighbor farmer in exchange for an old car that he had. He let me drive it but he said, "I won't sign the title over to you until the summer is over.' He also gave me a little spending money. It was enough to buy gas for the car and pay for my driver's license. I was really proud of my car. I called it "my old jalopy." Most of the other boys who graduated when I did didn't have a car yet. Mine wasn't paid for yet but I felt like I got ahead of the rest of them.

One day I was at the hardware store in town. A class mate that I graduated with was working at the hardware store. After talking for a while we started talking about fishing. I love to fish. At the hardware store they sold fishing tackle. He turned around and pulled a jar of fish bait off a shelf and set it on the counter. He tried to sell it to me. I didn't show much interest. He said, "They are salmon eggs. The fish really go for them." I said, "I'd rather fish with worms." He said, "But this bait will catch bigger fish than you will ever catch with a worm." I said, "I don't believe it." He said, "Just take it and try it. If you catch a big one with it, come back and pay me for it. If not, you don't owe me anything." I thought, "I can't go wrong on that." He said, "But you will need a big hook and some fifty pound test line." He talked me into buying that.

A little over a week later my boss let me have an afternoon off to go fishing. After digging some worms I went to the lake. I parked my old jalopy in the shade and baited my hook. I threw my line in the water and waited. Nothing happened. I tried another spot and then another spot. I wasn't getting any bites. Then I remembered the fish bait and tackle I got from my friend at the hardware store.

I thought "I can't have any worse luck with that than I'm having with my worms." I walked back to where my old jalopy was. I baited my hook again and threw it in the water. I left it in the water while I went to get the fishing tackle I got from the hardware store. I only had one fish reel so I tied an old spark plug on the end of the fifty pound test line, so I could swing it around and around my head and throw it out in the water. I put the big hook on the line.

When I popped the seal on that jar of fish bait an awful smell entered my nose. I almost gagged. I quickly put the lid back on again. I couldn't stand the smell. I remembered that I had a clothes pin in my old jalopy. I went and got it and clamped it on my nose before I opened the jar again. I'm sure people for miles around must have noted a strange smell when I opened that jar. I got out one of the things my friend called a salmon egg and put it on the hook. It didn't look like much on that big hook so I took out five more and threaded them onto the hook. I threw my line into the water and put the lid back on the jar before I took the clothes pin off my nose.

I put a stick through the spool of the fifty pound test line and stuck it into the ground. Then I went to check on my other fish line. I reeled it in and found I didn't have any more bait on my hook. I took it back to where my bait was. As I walked by the spool on the stick I noticed it was moving. I dropped my rod and reel and grabbed the spool. I soon realized I had something on my line. I pulled as hard as I could but I couldn't bring it in. I looked for a place to anchor the line. Then I saw my old jalopy parked near by. I let out enough line from the spool to be able to tie it around the back bumper of the jalopy. Then I got in and started the motor. I thought, "Now I'll show that fish who's in charge here." I put the car in gear and started to move forward. It didn't go far until it stopped moving. Then I suddenly realized I was moving backwards. I pushed the accelerator to the floor. I looked back and saw dirt and mud flying in the air from the back tires. Still I was moving backwards. As I was asking myself, "What do I do now?", I noticed that the car was in the water. When the water got up to the door I decided it was time to bail out. I waded back to dry ground and turned around to see what was happening. I saw the top of my old jalopy go under the water. That was the last I ever saw of it.

I started to walk the twelve miles back into town. When I got out to the highway a man stopped and picked me up. I expect that fish is still pulling my old jalopy around on the bottom of the lake. As you could guess, I never went back to pay for the stinken fish bait

Hybrid Chickens

My dad saw an advertisement in a farm magazine about hybrid chickens. The advertisement said, "They are bred to out produce any other chickens on the market." They didn't come cheap. I think he paid a dollar a piece for them. He ordered a hundred of them. They came in a perforated cardboard box. Instead of leaving them at the mail box, the mail man brought them to the house.

Dad had the brooder house ready for them when they arrived. When he turned them loose on the floor of the brooder house they ran around flapping their little wings. They were relieved to get out of that cramped up cardboard box. They were also glad for some food and water.

Since they were hybrids, we expected them to grow fast but they didn't. We wondered when the hybrid in them would start to show. After a month we still had 97 of them. Either my dad or my mom had accidentally stepped on three of them.

The hybrid in them didn't make any show until about a month after we got them. It manifested itself in an unusual way. I swept up all their droppings and loaded them in a wheel barrow. I took them out and spread them on the garden. The next morning I saw an amazing phenomenon in the garden. All the plants were standing up strong and tall with color they didn't have before. Tomato plants shot up waist high. We had to set a post beside each tomato plant and tie it up. When we picked the snap beans they were six to eight inches long. Watermelon vines started spreading out beyond the limits of the garden.

We discovered we had a gold mine in chicken manure. We gave some to our neighbors and they had the same results. Someone suggested that we should commercialize it. We put an ad in the local paper. Word got around and people from miles around started coming to buy chicken manure. The chickens couldn't produce it fast enough to meet the demand. I took a putty knife and scrapped ever speck of it off the floor. As the chickens grew older they produced a little more manure but they still couldn't keep up with the demand.

It wasn't unusual to have water melons that weighed fifty or sixty pounds. We had to take a step ladder to the garden to pick the tomatoes. The carrots grew waist high with roots that measured six inches in diameter. That year we took all the prizes at the county fair in the fresh produce division.

When the chickens got old enough to butcher we didn't even think of killing them. They were making us rich by the manure they were producing. When the chickens were around four months old disaster struck. They turned to cannibalism. I mean they started eating one another. I'll never know what made them do that. They fought one another to the death and then ate all the meat off the bones. Within the space of two weeks all we had left was one rooster. He was mean. He preferred human flesh to the best commercial chicken feed. We decided we would have to get rid of him. No one wanted to catch him because he would take out big chunks of flesh with his sharp beak I took a fishing net and captured him with it. While I stood on the handle of the net my sister tied a heavy cord around the net so he couldn't get out. We found a unique way to get rid of him. We put the rooster, still tied in the fishing net, in the back of the pickup and took him to the house of a neighbor who had a small plane. He took me up in his plane with the rooster tied in the fishing net. When we got up around a thousand feet I opened the door of the plane and extended the net out the door. I took a pair of scissors and cut the cord. The rooster fell out and began flapping his wings, thinking he would fly back to the ground. It wasn't long before he folded up his wings and fell to the ground. No doubt some coyote feasted on his remains.